LEVELLING UP LEFT BEHIND PLACES

THE SCALE AND NATURE OF THE ECONOMIC AND POLICY CHALLENGE

RON MARTIN, BEN GARDINER, ANDY PIKE,
PETER SUNLEY AND PETER TYLER

Regional Studies Policy Impact Books
Series Editor: Louise Kempton

RSA **Regional Studies**
Association

Research Today, Policy Tomorrow

First published 2021
by Taylor & Francis
4 Park Square, Milton Park, Abingdon, Oxon, OX14 4RN

Taylor & Francis Group, an informa business

British Library Cataloguing-in-Publication Data
A catalogue record for this book is available from the British Library.

Trademark notice: Product or corporate names may be trademarks or registered trademarks, and are used only for identification and explanation without intent to infringe.

ISBN13: 978-1-032-24430-3 (print)
ISBN13: 978-1-032-24434-1 (e-book)

Typeset in 10.5/13.5 Myriad Pro
by Nova Techset Private Limited, Bengaluru and Chennai, India

Disclosure statement: No potential conflict of interest was reported by the authors.

Please visit https://taylorandfrancis.com/about/corporate-responsibility/accessibility-at-taylor-francis/ for further information on the accessibility features available for Regional Studies Policy Impact Books

CONTENTS

LEVELLING UP LEFT BEHIND PLACES

The scale and nature of the economic and policy challenge

FOREWORD

Addressing the gap in employment and incomes, in opportunities, between and within different places, has become the defining challenge in UK politics and policy, as in some other Western countries. As this important contribution demonstrates, the policies implemented during the past four decades have—at best—failed to limit or reduce spatial inequalities, while some (such as infrastructure investments and privatizations) have helped increase them. Yet policy, active intervention by the state, is the only way to level up, given the spillovers and market failures inherent in the process of economic growth. Understanding why previous policies have failed and ensuring new ones learn from past experience is therefore essential, making this book so timely.

One key issue is being clear about the extent of dispersion between and within different geographies, acknowledging the economic and political complexity involved. The gap in median earnings or gross value added (GVA) per capita between regions is sometimes overstated in public debate when only a part of London is used to stand for the whole; but on the other hand, almost all the UK's highest earners are in the capital. Correspondingly, the inequalities within regions are sometimes under-emphasized, glossed over in a "North versus South" debate, and yet for many policymakers in subnational government these are a higher priority. People living in some areas of multiple deprivation are those most in need of effective "levelling up" policies, in terms of health and longevity as well as more direct economic outcomes. There is a pressing need to better understand these inequalities and how they have evolved over time, and this book seeks to meet this need.

A second set of issues concerns the institutional and governance framework in the UK. The top-down tradition in policymaking and the frequent policy reversals—even during the same government—makes the development and implementation of spatial policies dysfunctional. The centre has no means of gathering the essential, granular information generated by other countries' more bottom-up policy processes. There is no institutional longevity in policy development and implementation, and hence no mechanism for learning from what

https://doi.org/10.1080/2578711X.2021.1992161
© 2021 Ron Martin, Ben Gardiner, Andy Pike, Peter Sunley and
Peter Tyler

has (or has not) happened previously. There is nothing enabling the coordination of policies, across ministries and across localities, so essential to bring about change in the structure of the economy, aside from the blunt veto power of HM Treasury. Further devolution of powers from Westminster and Whitehall (and in a more meaningful way than shipping a few hundred national civil servants to towns in the Midlands and North of England) is one obvious requirement. But the centre itself lacks necessary institutional capabilities for the strategic management of the national economy, including its geographical distribution.

The UK faced these significant challenges before March 2020, having experienced stagnant productivity and growth since the 2008 global financial crisis. The Covid-19 pandemic has made them more acute, having exacerbated all the spatial inequalities scarring our society. It has also made us more aware of the likelihood of further crises, whether future pandemics, climate-related extreme weather, technological disruptions or other shocks unimagined. The questions addressed in this book, therefore, could not be more important or urgent, and both the analysis and policy issues discussed herein make a key contribution to the "levelling up" debate.

Diane Coyle
Bennett Professor of Public Policy,
University of Cambridge, Cambridge, UK
dc700@cam.ac.uk

ABOUT THE AUTHORS

Ron Martin is Emeritus Professor of Economic Geography at the University of Cambridge, and Emeritus Professorial Fellow of St Catharine's College, University of Cambridge, UK. From 2015 to 2020, he was President of the Regional Studies Association (RSA). He is also a Research Associate of the Centre for Business Research, Judge Business School, University of Cambridge. Ron has published some 25 books and more than 275 journal papers on economic geography, regional and urban development, the economic resilience of regions and cities, the geographies of money and finance, and spatial policy. He has undertaken research for the European Commission, the Organisation for Economic Co-operation and Development (OECD), the UK government, and national and regional institutions. He is a Fellow of the Academy of Social Sciences and a Fellow of the British Academy. In 2016, he was awarded the Royal Geographical Society's (RGS) Victoria Gold Medal for his "outstanding contributions to economic geography". In 2018 and in 2021, he was selected as a "Highly Cited Researcher" by the Web of Science.
✉ rlm1@cam.ac.uk; 🄳 0000-0002-6203-0518

Ben Gardiner is a Director and Chief Operating Officer of Cambridge Econometrics (CE), Cambridge, UK. He holds a doctorate in economic geography from the University of Cambridge, UK. His interests are in regional and city economic growth across Europe, regional productivity, and the economic resilience of regions and cities. He has been involved with several Economic and Social Research Council (ESRC) projects on regional and city economic growth and transformation. For several years, he was a Research Associate in the Department of Geography, University of Cambridge, and has also worked for the European Commission (DG JRC-Seville) on its regional "RHOMOLO Model" of Cohesion Funds.
✉ bg@camecon.com

Andy Pike is the Henry Daysh Professor of Regional Development Studies, Newcastle University, UK. From 2012 to 2017, he was Director of the Centre for Urban and Regional Development Studies (CURDS), Newcastle University. His research interests, publications and research projects are focused on the geographical political economy of local, regional, and urban development and policy. He has undertaken research projects for the OECD, United

Nations International Labour Organization (UN-ILO), European Commission, UK government, and national, regional and local institutions. He is a Fellow of the Regional Studies Association (RSA) and a Fellow of the Academy of Social Sciences.

✉ andy.pike@newcastle.ac.uk; 🆔 0000-0001-7651-2983

Peter Sunley is Professor of Economic Geography and formerly Director of Research and Enterprise at the University of Southampton, UK. His research has focused on geographies of labour and labour market policy, business clusters and venture capital, design and creative industries, urban development and resilience, and manufacturing in industrial regions. He is a member of the Research Committee of the Regional Studies Association (RSA) and a Fellow of the Academy of Social Sciences.

✉ p.j.sunley@soton.ac.uk; 🆔 0000-0003-4803-5299

Peter Tyler is Emeritus Professor of Urban and Regional Economics at the University of Cambridge, and Emeritus Professorial Fellow of St Catharine's College, University of Cambridge, UK. His research interests cover the economics of regions and cities, regional policy, and urban planning, with a special focus on public policy impacts. He has directed over 70 regional and urban research projects for the UK government, many of which have involved the evaluation of flagship policy programmes. He has also been an Expert Advisor to the Organisation for Economic Co-operation and Development (OECD), the European Commission, and the UK government, and, in 2016, was Expert Advisor to United Nations' Habitat III. Peter is a Member of the Royal Town Planning Institute (RTPI), a Fellow of the Royal Institute of Chartered Surveyors (RICS) and a Fellow of the Academy of Social Sciences.

✉ pt23@cam.ac.uk; 🆔 0000-0002-9299-5396

ACKNOWLEDGEMENTS

The authors are grateful to the Regional Studies Association (RSA) for commissioning this book, and for its support in funding the research on which it is based. Some of the arguments and findings also draw on our various other related projects. These include: *How Regions React to Recessions: Resilience, Hysteresis and Long-Run Impacts* (grant number ES/1035811/1); *Structural Transformation, Adaptability and City Economic Evolutions* (grant number ES/N006135/1); *Manufacturing Renaissance in Industrial Regions? Investigating the Potential of Advanced Manufacturing for Sectoral and Spatial Rebalancing* (grant number ES/P003923/1), and *Beyond Left Behind Places* (grant number ES/V013696/1), all funded by the Economic and Social Research Council (ESRC). The views expressed herein are of course entirely our own, and do not necessarily reflect those of the RSA.

https://doi.org/10.1080/2578711X.2021.1992162
© 2021 Ron Martin, Ben Gardiner, Andy Pike, Peter Sunley and Peter Tyler

PREAMBLE

This book aims to understand the economic predicament of "left behind places" and how their weaknesses have been shaped by changes in the national and international economy, deindustrialization, and the transition to service-dominated economies. Crucially, it focuses on the distinctive economic experiences of different types of left behind places in the UK, although many of the findings and arguments are of wider international relevance. The key features of urban and regional institutions and policies are reviewed to understand more about why, despite some successes, geographical economic inequalities remain an entrenched feature of the UK, blighting the life chances and quality of life of its citizens, and national economic progress as a whole.

https://doi.org/10.1080/2578711X.2021.1992163
© 2021 Ron Martin, Ben Gardiner, Andy Pike, Peter Sunley and Peter Tyler

EXECUTIVE SUMMARY AND KEY RECOMMENDATIONS

The nature of the problem:

- Geographical inequalities in the UK are a longstanding and persistent problem rooted in deep-seated and cumulative processes of local and regional divergence with antecedents in the inter-war years and accelerating since the early 1980s.

- This spatial divergence has been generated by the inability of some places to adapt to the emergence of the post-industrial service and knowledge-based economy whose geographies are very different from those of past heavy industries. As a consequence, *the "left behind" problem has become spatially and systemically entrenched.*

- Challenging ideas of market-led adjustment, there is little evidence that real cost advantages in Northern areas are correcting and offsetting the geographically differentiated development of skilled labour and human capital and the quality of residential and business environments.

- A variety of different types of "left behind place" exist at different scales, and these types combine common problems with distinctive economic trajectories and varied causes. *These different types will need policies that are sensitive and adaptive to their specific problems and potentialities.*

- Contemporary economic development is marked by agglomeration in high-skilled and knowledge-intensive activities. Research-based concentrations of high-skilled activity in the UK have been limited and concentrated heavily in parts of London and cities in the Golden Triangle, especially Oxford and Cambridge. *Even in London, the benefits have been unevenly spread between boroughs.*

- Existing analyses of the predicaments of left behind places present a stark division between rapid growth in "winning" high-skilled cities and relative decline in "losing" areas. This view is problematic because it oversimplifies the experience in the UK and other countries. *A false binary distinction is presented to policymakers which offers only the possibility of growth in larger cities and derived spillovers and other compensations elsewhere.*

https://doi.org/10.1080/2578711X.2021.1992164
© 2021 Ron Martin, Ben Gardiner, Andy Pike, Peter Sunley and Peter Tyler

- Yet, the post-industrial economy involves strong dispersal of activity and growth to smaller cities, towns and rural areas. However, this process has been highly selective between local areas and needs to be better understood.

The institutional and policy response:

- *Past policies in the UK have lacked recognition of the scale and importance of the left behind problem and committed insufficient resources to its resolution.* The objective of achieving a less geographically unequal economy has not been incorporated into mainstream policymaking. When compared with other countries, the UK has taken an overcentralized, "top-down" approach to policy formulation and implementation, often applying "one size fits all" policy measures to different geographical situations.

- *Political cycles have underpinned a disruptive churn of institutions and policies.* In contrast with other Organisation for Economic Co-operation and Development (OECD) countries, particularly in Europe, there has been limited long-term strategy and continuity, and inadequate development of local policymaking capacity and capabilities, especially for research, analysis, monitoring and evaluation.

- *Past policies have been underfunded, inconsistent, and inadequately tailored and adapted to the needs of different local economies.* We estimate that, on average over the period 1961–2020, the UK government invested on average £2.9 billion per annum in direct spatial policy (2020 prices), equivalent to around 0.15% of gross national income (GNI) per annum over the period. European Union Structural and Cohesion Policy support has added around 0.12% GNI (2020 prices) per annum to this over the period from the late 1970s.

- These broad estimates suggest that discretionary expenditure in the UK on urban and regional policy when both domestic and European Union spatial policy was in operation was equivalent to 0.27% per annum of UK GNI (2020 prices). This is dwarfed by mainstream spending programmes (by comparison, the UK committed £14.5 billion (0.7% of GNI) to international aid in 2019). The level of resources devoted to spatial policy has been modest given the entrenched and cumulative nature of the problem.

- *Policies for "levelling up" need clearly to distinguish different types of left behind places and devise a set of place-sensitive and targeted policies for these types of "clubs" of left behind areas.* This shift will need a radical expansion of "place-based" policymaking in the UK which allows national and local actors to collaborate on the design of appropriate targeted programmes.

- *A key priority for "levelling up" is revitalizing Northern cities and boosting their contribution to the national economy.* Underperformance in these urban centres has been a major contributor to persistent geographical inequality in the UK.

- Addressing the UK's geographical economic inequalities and the plight of left behind places *requires substantially more decentralization of power and resources to place-based agencies.* This would enable the current UK government's "levelling up" agenda to capitalize on the many advantages of more "place-based" policymaking to diagnose problems, build on local capabilities, strengthen resilience and adapt to local changes in circumstances.

- *Crucially, place-based efforts need to be coordinated and aligned with place-sensitive national policies.* The key challenge of a levelling up mission is to integrate "place-based" policies with greater place sensitivity in national policies and in regulation and mainstream economic spending.

- It is important to *develop policies that spread the benefits from agglomeration* and ensure that the income effects and innovations produced by high-skill concentrations diffuse to the wider city-regional economies and their firms (especially small and medium-sized enterprises) and workers. There is a clear need for more policy thinking on how this can be achieved.

- *Policy for levelling-up needs to align and coordinate with the other national missions for net zero carbon and post-pandemic recovery.* This suggests that a strong "place-making" agenda focused on quality of life, infrastructure and housing in many left behind places is important for post-industrial and service growth.

- Genuine place-making is a long-term process involving public, private and civic participation which allows local responses to those economic, environmental, and social constraints and problems that most strongly reduce the quality of life in local areas. *A truly "total place" approach is required.* The quality of infrastructure, housing stock and public services is crucial for the quality of place as well as the ability to secure and attract more dispersed forms of growth. There is little hope of delivering "place-making" if public sector austerity is once again allowed to cut back public services more severely in poorer and more deprived areas.

The way forward:

- The scale and nature of the UK's contemporary "left behind places" problem are such that only a transformative shift in policy model and a resource commitment of historic proportions are likely to achieve the "levelling up" ambition that is central to the current government's political ambitions.

KEY RECOMMENDATIONS

In summary, our recommendations are that the UK government should:

- Grasp the transformative moment for local, regional and urban development policy as the UK adjusts to a post-Covid-19 world and seeks a net zero carbon future.

- Establish a clear and binding national mission for "levelling up".

- Realize the potential of place in policymaking.

- Decentralize and devolve towards a multilevel federal polity.

- Strengthen subnational funding and financing and adopt new financing models involving the public, private sector and civic sectors to generate the resources required.

- Embed geography in the national state and in national policy machinery.

- Improve subnational strategic research, intelligence, monitoring and evaluation capacity.

A failure to learn from the lessons of the last 70 years of spatial policy risks the UK becoming an ever more divided nation, with all the associated economic, social and political costs, risks and challenges that this presents.

https://doi.org/10.1080/2578711X.2021.1992164

1. INTRODUCTION: THE NEW DISCOURSE OF "LEFT BEHIND PLACES"

Keywords: left behind places, levelling up, discontent

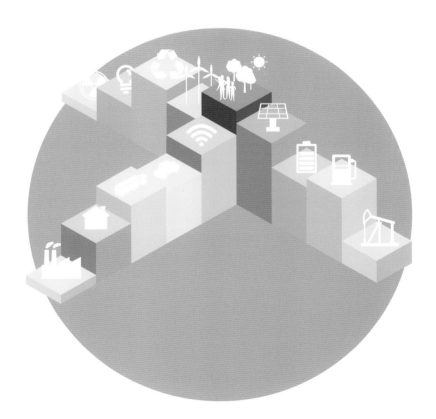

1.1 THE RE-EMERGENCE AND (RE)DISCOVERY OF "LEFT BEHIND PLACES"

In the space of just over a decade, the world economy has experienced two dramatic disruptions that are only supposed to be "once-in-a-century" events: first, the global financial crisis of 2007–08, and the great recession this triggered; and second, the global Covid-19 pandemic that began in late 2019, and the great economic lockdown this engendered as states sought to control its spread. Both events have exposed and highlighted pronounced spatial inequalities in economic prosperity and welfare. Inequalities have both shaped the uneven impact of these historic shocks and economic recovery strategies in the wake of these complex, momentous and unprecedented challenges.

The fact of the matter, however, is that spatial inequalities had been widening in several of the advanced economies, including the United States, the UK and various European Union states well before the global financial crisis and pandemic, although compounded and intensified still further by them.[2] Cities and regions around the world have been struggling to formulate responses and recovery plans.

For much of the post-war period, up to the late 1970s or early 1980s, in many advanced countries there had been a slow but progressive narrowing of spatial inequalities, and a trend towards regional and local economic convergence. But since then, over the past four decades, both social and regional and local economic convergence has ceased, and in several instances has even been replaced by divergence as spatial inequalities have widened. While the precise timing, scale and geographical specifics of this growth in spatial inequality vary from country to country, the basic outcome is similar: major gaps have opened up between successful places that have "pulled ahead" economically and places that have failed to share in the same success (Box 1.1). In the period since the 2008 crash, these latter areas have become characterized in both academic studies and political discourse as "left behind places". This is an international phenomenon, with national and subnational particularities, for example, "La France périphérique" (peripheral France), "abgehängte Regionen" (suspended regions) in Germany, "Aree Interne" (inner areas) in Italy, "Krimpgebieden" (shrinking areas) in the Netherlands, "la España vaciada" (the hollowed out Spain), and "legacy cities" and the "rustbelt" in the United States.

In fact, the notion of the "left behind" is not new. It has been used for decades in social and political discourses as a way of invoking a collective moral responsibility for helping disadvantaged

Regional Studies Policy Impact Books

https://doi.org/10.1080/2578711X.2021.1992165
© 2020 Ron Martin, Ben Gardiner, Andy Pike, Peter Sunley and Peter Tyler

> **Box 1.1 Rising regional inequalities**
>
> Within their own borders, OECD [Organisation for Economic Co-operation and Development] countries are witnessing increasing gaps in GDP [gross domestic product] per capita between higher performing and lower performing regions. … The gaps within countries between the top 10% regions with the highest productivity and the bottom 75% has grown on average by about 60% over the last two decades.[3]
>
> It is remarkable that the emerging picture on regional inequality in the long-run is also similar to the pattern of inequality in terms of personal income and wealth distributions … the pattern of regional inequality [in Europe] over the last 110 years follows a U-shape, just like the pattern of personal income inequality … after 1900 we find a spread of economic activity across regions and convergence until about 1980, and divergence as well as geographical re-concentration thereafter.[4]

groups in society. It signals a collective responsibility to ensure that those who are disadvantaged in some way are not abandoned to their fates. The phrase was used explicitly in the United States' No Child Left Behind Act 2001, which was concerned with targeting federal assistance to raise the educational attainment of children in economically and socially disadvantaged ("left behind") families. Traditionally, the notion of being "left behind" has strongly associated disadvantage with immobility and people staying in place. Indeed, the primary area in which the term has been used is in migration studies. Many migration studies have been concerned with the problems of areas of strong outmigration, where often elderly and less well qualified groups have been left behind by the movement away of younger, more ambitious groups in search of opportunities elsewhere. Some studies continue to use the phrase "left-behind" to refer specifically to declining rural areas and small towns that have suffered decades of population loss and self-perpetuating endemic problems of poverty and low skills.[5]

In recent years the "left behind" idea has been extended into new debates and become used as a label for a much broader variety of relatively disadvantaged and deprived places and communities. A key document here was the World Bank's Development Report *Reshaping Economic Geography* (2009), which stressed the economic benefits of urban density, agglomeration and integration. It argued that:

> As the world's economy grows, people and production are concentrating, pulled as if by gravity to prosperous places—growing cities, leading areas, and connected countries. As it did decades ago in today's high-income countries, the drive to density in low- and middle-income countries can increase the sense of deprivation as the economic distance between prosperous areas and those left behind widens.[6]

The report aligns economic success with integration and movement to cities and contrasts this with places that have failed to react to or benefit from the "gravitational" pull of cities.

In this way, the notion of "left behind places" began to gain a wider meaning to refer to less urbanized and deprived localities.

In some ways echoing this World Bank view, in the United States the pull of dynamic cities has figured prominently in discussions of what has been called a "great divergence", a growing gap between, at one extreme, so-called "brain hub" or "super star" cities that have attracted large numbers of highly educated, skilled and well-paid workers, and, at the other extreme, former manufacturing cities that have rapidly lost jobs and residents.[7] In between are cities that are judged able to go either way in their future development trajectories. Other commentators similarly refer to the emergence of "a dramatic gap between 'two Americas', one based in large, diverse, thriving metropolitan regions; the other found in more homogeneous small towns and rural areas struggling under the weight of economic stagnation and social decline".[8] Still others characterize the problem as a divergence between two "separate regional worlds", one of which has enjoyed the benefits of globalization and technological advance, and another that has failed to share in those benefits and which instead has borne the brunt of the disruptive impacts that globalization and technological change have inevitably entailed.[9]

In Europe, the picture is broadly similar, though necessarily varied and complex because of differences between countries in economic structures, governance arrangements, varying dates of entry into the European Union, and other nationally and regionally specific factors. Nevertheless, overall, across much of Europe regional economic inequalities have also widened since circa 1980.[10] Like the United States, Europe has seen diverging fortunes among its rural regions, towns and cities. Growth in industrial output has tended to be stronger in the countryside and towns than in the major cities of Western Europe. But high-value and high-wage services and technology sectors have become more concentrated in particular metropolitan regions, and especially in capital cities.[11]

In the UK, geographical inequalities in economic performance and prosperity have also widened since the late 1970s and have proved particularly problematic.[12] However, the problem differs in some key respects from that in the United States, in that, with the very important exception of London, the national capital, the country's major cities have not been amongst the places that have "pulled ahead".[13] Most of the largest cities—and almost all former major industrial centres—are in the "northern" half of the country. Indeed, in the 1980s, a fierce debate emerged around the opening up of a major geographical fault line between a more prosperous and dynamic "South" and a less prosperous and economically lagging "North", what was in fact the reassertion of a "North–South divide" that in some fundamental aspects can be traced back to the mid-19th century.[14]

In the wake of the 2007–09 financial crisis, this "North–South" problem of regional economic inequality was relabelled as one of "spatial imbalance", of an economy that had become too dependent on just a few sectors of activity, especially finance, and overly

Regional Studies Policy Impact Books   https://doi.org/10.1080/2578711X.2021.1992165

concentrated in London and its South East hinterland. The policy challenge, framed by national government, was that of "rebalancing" the economy, spatially and sectorally, by "powering up" Northern cities.[15] But barely a decade later, in the context of the UK's exit from the European Union and the General Election of 2019, the political language used to characterize the problem and its policy challenge had been changed again by national government to one of "levelling up" the places that had been economically "left behind". In the UK, and elsewhere internationally, this notion of "levelling up" has become a prominent policy mantra. It is attractive to politicians and policymakers in seeming to address the plight of the "left behind places" while not holding back the advance of the more prosperous cities and regions. Yet, beyond its invocation as a political catchphrase, what is actually meant by "levelling up" remains vague and widely criticized for being more a political slogan than a clear strategy with well-specified aims and policy programmes.

1.2 "LEFT BEHIND PLACES" AS SITES OF DISCONTENT

Reviving "left behind places"—improving their economic performance and prosperity, and social and environmental conditions—wherever they are, is a problem that politicians and policymakers can ill-afford to ignore. Across several of the advanced Organisation for Economic Co-operation and Development (OECD) countries, the voting populations in "left behind places" either feel forgotten by mainstream politicians and their policies, or at worst deliberately neglected by them in favour of the more prosperous places and the metropolitan centres and capitals that are driving economic growth and where national political and economic elites are typically concentrated. This sentiment has fostered an uneven "geography of discontent" in Europe and elsewhere.[16]

The electorates in many "left behind places" have seen the ballot box as a means of expressing their dissatisfaction and disillusionment with their lagging fortunes and diminishing opportunities. While the recent rise of political populism and economic nationalism in many countries has many causes, and has involved new movements on both the right and left of the political spectrum, there is no doubt that such interests can be seen, in part at least, as acts of "revenge" by those living in the places left behind by the economic progress of recent decades.[17]

In the United States, Donald Trump owed his 2016 presidential election success in part to playing to this geography of "abandoned places", and the grievances of their residents, with his populist agenda of economic nationalism to restrict globalization, revive traditional industries, and "bring jobs back" to the country's economically lagging towns and cities (Box 1.2).

Trump's claim was that many of the job losses in these areas have been due to the failure of previous US administrations to protect American interests and prevent jobs being moved overseas. While the 2020 Presidential Election winner may have changed, the nation's

> **Box 1.2 The problem of "abandoned places" in the United States**
>
> Right now, 92 million Americans are on the side-lines, outside the workforce, and not part of our economy. It's a silent nation of jobless Americans. Look no further than the city of Flint, where I just visited. The jobs have stripped from this community, and its infrastructure has collapsed. In 1970, there were more than 80,000 people in Flint working for GM—today it is less than 8,000. Now Ford has announced it is moving all small car production to Mexico. It used to be cars that were made in Flint and you couldn't drink the water in Mexico. Now, the cars are made in Mexico and you can't drink the water in Flint. … In many parts of our country, the hard times never seem to end.[18]

economic and political geography remains rigidly divided. As Muro et al. put it, the US political–economic map:

> continues to reflect a striking split between the large, dense, metropolitan counties that voted Democratic and the mostly exurban, small-town, or rural counties that voted Republican. Blue and red America reflect two very different economies: one oriented to diverse, often college-educated workers in professional and digital services occupations, and the other whiter, less-educated, and more dependent on "traditional" industries.[19]

In the UK, by the time of the Brexit vote in 2016, it was evident that the problem of longstanding and persistent spatial inequalities was not just economic in nature, but involved unexpected shifts in the map of political sentiment and allegiance. Jennings and Stoker describe a bifurcation of politics between cosmopolitan and liberal areas of growth, and "provincial backwaters" marked by weak economies and illiberal and nostalgic attitudes. In this stark view, economic polarization is driving political polarization.[20] The Brexit vote in 2016, and then especially the 2019 election of the Conservative government led by Prime Minister Boris Johnson, certainly owed much to the support of the less prosperous industrial cities, towns and localities in the Midlands and North of England. Many of these were constituencies that had traditionally voted Labour (the so-called "red wall" constituencies), but which now switched allegiance to the Conservatives with their promise to "get Brexit done" and to "level up" the country. The irony was that many of these very same areas had suffered disproportionately from a decade of austerity since 2010 and for years had benefited from European Union aid and investment.

Many poorer parts of the country have also borne the brunt of the Covid-19 pandemic. As the UK, like other countries, resorted to the imposition of strict social and economic lockdowns in order to control the spread of the virus, so the economy plummeted into a downturn that was even deeper than that triggered by the global financial crisis. The collapse of economic output—of some 20.4% in the second quarter of 2020, and of 9.9% for 2020 as a whole—was the worst on historical record. Both Covid infection rates and economic

https://doi.org/10.1080/2578711X.2021.1992165

contraction have been highest in the least prosperous areas of the country, many of which are in the North. The economic structures and jobs in such places contain relatively higher levels of key workers in essential public services and those in lower paid activities such as care, logistics and transportation, more exposed to viral transmission and less able to isolate or work from home. What the Covid-19 pandemic has done, in all the advanced economies, not just the UK, is to further expose and intensify spatial inequalities that had been developing for some time previously.

This stark reality has accentuated the need for political action to "level up" the social and economic conditions in the "left behind" places, an imperative that has featured in almost all of Prime Minister Johnson's policy speeches and statements, including his New Deal for Britain (2020) and Build Back Better (2021) plans for recovery from the post-Covid recession (Box 1.3). As Chapter 6 elaborates, this policy agenda includes the introduction of a number of nationally administered centralized grant-funding initiatives with specific geographical foci across the UK, including the Community Renewal Fund, Levelling Up Fund, Towns Fund and promised Shared Prosperity Fund (to be launched in 2022). Other policy goals are also intended to support the government's "levelling up agenda". Thus, the legal commitment to achieve net zero carbon by 2050 is supposed to be targeted at "green" investment and projects "in the UK's industrial heartlands, including in the North East, Yorkshire and the Humber, West Midlands, Scotland and Wales, which will drive forward the green industrial "revolution and build green jobs and industries of the future".[21] Another initiative is the long-awaited "National Infrastructure Strategy", which states that "levelling up is [the] government's core purpose" and that the strategy "will significantly shift spending to the regions and nations of the UK".[22]

Box 1.3 The "levelling up" of the UK's economic geography

[T]oo many parts of this country have felt left behind. Neglected, unloved, as though someone had taken a strategic decision that their fate did not matter as much as the metropolis [London]. So I want you to know that this government not only has a vision to change this for the better. We have a mission to unite and to level up. … We will double down on levelling up. … We will unleash the potential of the entire country. … To mend the indefensible gap in opportunity and productivity and connectivity between the regions of the UK. … We will not just bounce back. We will bounce forward—stronger and better and more united than ever before.[23]

Just as the government has done whatever it takes to support lives and livelihoods throughout the Covid crisis, so we will turn that same ambition and resolve to the task of our recovery. We will level up our country, so the map of our whole United Kingdom is lit up with competitive cities and vibrant towns that are centres of life—places people are proud to call home, with access to the services and the jobs they need to thrive.[24]

1.3 WHAT ARE "LEFT BEHIND PLACES"?

The policy challenge of addressing the problem of "left behind places" through "levelling up" national economic geographies, whether in the United States, UK or elsewhere, is not only daunting but also problematic. To begin with, there is the basic question of what exactly do we mean by "left behind"? While some apply the term to areas showing the strongest political discontent or dissatisfaction, others use it to highlight areas of greatest economic disadvantage. Despite their strong connections, the two definitions do not, of course, always neatly correspond. There is no single, agreed-upon definition of the notion, nor of the criteria that should be used to identify "left behind places". Such places could be defined in economic, or social, or health or environmental terms. These different metrics may, or may not, result in the same areas being designated "left behind". And what are the reference points, or "benchmarks", against which being "left behind" is judged: a national average position, an agreed minimum standard, or other such benchmark or target? How far below an agreed reference point does a place have to be to qualify as "left behind"?

Some studies and discussions have sought to define and identify "left behind" places by collating various indicators of local economic and social conditions—such as wages, incomes, housing conditions, employment rates, unemployment rates, skills, educational attainments, health outcomes, access to public amenities, etc.—and then combining these into some sort of composite index of socio-economic disadvantage. In the UK, this approach has been used for some time to construct local indices of deprivation (IoDs) and indices of multiple deprivation (IMDs) for small areas, from individual neighbourhoods to postcode districts, to local authorities, all of which can then be ranked according to their scores. National and local organizations use the IoD, often in conjunction with other data, to distribute funding or target resources to individual areas. It is widely used across central government to focus programmes on the most deprived areas. Local authorities have also used it as evidence in the development of strategies, to focus interventions and in bids for funding. The voluntary and community sector also uses the IoD, for example, to identify areas where people may benefit from the community and other services they provide. A key limitation of using official IoDs to define "left behind" places, however, is that the index is not intended to provide "backwards" comparisons through time.[25]

Nevertheless, a similar approach has been applied in an attempt to give empirical rigour to the "left behind" problem. Davenport and Zaranko, for example, suggest a range of economic and multiple deprivation statistics to identify a variety of different types of "left behind place".[26] Others have used a range of indicators to argue that only "certain types" of deprived area are in fact "left behind". In this approach, these areas should not just be defined on the basis of economic weaknesses, but if they also show very poor public, educational, civic association and community assets, poor infrastructure, and inadequate transport services. According to the Local Trust, for example, "left behind" neighbourhoods are those that appear in the bottom

10% of neighbourhoods on both deprivation and community need indices, so that they are a specific subset of deprived places where the lack of services and facilities do not connect people and bind them together.[27] Such services underline how local disadvantage is multidimensional and economic problems are often compounded by an erosion of social, community, cultural, and environmental capital and resources.[28]

However, combinations of several indicators, particularly at the scale of regions, cities and towns, should in fact be treated with much caution and careful examination. For one thing, at scales above the very local (e.g., neighbourhoods), there may not be close correlation between the different indicators used: a place might be defined as "deprived" (or "left behind") on one indicator but not necessarily on another. Further, there is also the issue of what weights should be given to the various individual indicators used to derive a composite index: different weights may well produce a different set, or ranking, of "left behind" places and a different geography of public support and funding. In its methodology for operationalizing its Levelling Up Fund, the UK government has focused on five main indicators for categorizing the country's 370 local authority districts (LADs) into three priority tiers: local productivity, unemployment rate, skills, transport connectivity and property vacancy rates (Table 1.1). Combining these indicators into a "need for recovery index" yields 123 LADs in the top priority tier. In this approach, however, transport and property indicators are given equal weight to

Table 1.1 Identifying "left behind places" for "levelling up" funding in the UK: "index to capture the need for economic recovery across British local authority areas"

Target metric	Indicator	Data year	Indicator weight (%)
A. Main indicators			Total 50%
Local productivity	log Gross value added (GVA) per hour worked	2018	16.7%
Local unemployment	Rate (%) for over 16-year-olds	October 2019–September 2020	16.7%
Local skills	Proportion of 16–64-year-old population without National Vocational Qualifications (NVQs) or formal education	2019	16.7%
B. Additional indicators			Total 50%
Need for improved transport connectivity	Average journey time to employment centres, by mode	2020	25.0%
Need for regeneration	Commercial and dwelling vacancy rates	2020	25.0%

Source: UK Government (2021) *Levelling Up Fund: Prioritisation of Places Methodology Note*, tab. 1. https://www.gov.uk/government/publications/levelling-up-fund-additional-documents/levelling-up-fund-prioritisation-of-places-methodology-note

three "main" economic criteria, and the "journey time to employment centres" statistic will inevitably raise the scores for remote towns and rural areas.

As we will show in Chapters 2 and 3, the problem of spatial inequality is complex, compound and multi-scalar. The "left behind place" debate has suffered from a lack of clarity about these scales, and it has frequently privileged a single scale and conflated problems and causes at one scale with those at larger or smaller scales. Not only have some broad regions failed to match the growth in living standards in other regions, but also there are marked, often greater, intra-regional inequalities, so that some places have "fallen behind" compared with their neighbours within the same region. Even within relatively affluent local areas some neighbourhoods have been "left behind", as has been shown by recent work on "nested deprivation".[29] Local inequalities are substantial in some prosperous urban areas. Given that "left behind" places exist at different scales, and can be defined in different ways, any effective programme of responding to these issues will demand an integrated and coordinated set of different policies at different scales.

Yet further, most attempts to identify "left behind places" are typically based on static cross-section metrics and indicators measured at one moment in time (or as near to the same point in time as possible): this is exemplified by the UK's Levelling Up Fund methodology (Table 1.1). This may give an indication of regional and local inequalities, say in per capita incomes or productivity, as a snapshot at that moment in time, but it indicates little about how those spatial inequalities have come into being, or how they have been evolving. In other words, they fail to reveal much about a region's or locality's "direction of travel", how it has come to be "left behind" and in what ways. In addition, this issue is compounded by the fact that there are likely to be different sorts of "left behind places", with different locally specific problems and causal histories. Thus, while two localities may have a similar score on the particular index or metric chosen to identify "left behind places", the reasons for their having low scores may differ considerably. Hence, understanding the scale, nature and geographies of the "left behind" problem requires illuminating the differential growth and development paths of places that have brought them to their current situation, to identify just how far and why they have "fallen behind" in relation to more prosperous places. This highlights "levelling up" as an ongoing analytical and policy challenge.

1.4. "LEVELLING UP": MOVING BEYOND SLOGANS

What, precisely, then does "levelling up" mean? Without sufficient clarity the danger is that it resembles more of a political slogan than a well-specified objective and policy strategy, the outcomes of which are capable of being monitored and assessed. The problem is that it is a notion, an objective, that is far from easy to pin down.[30] As the UK Institute of Fiscal Studies

> **Box 1.4 The complexity of the "left behind" and "levelling up" problems**
>
> The UK's regional inequalities are deep-rooted and complex: even well-designed policies could take years or even decades to have meaningful effects. "Levelling up" will need to be a long-term, multifaceted agenda if it is to succeed where other governments have failed in the past. ... There is no single set of factors that characterise a "left-behind" place. In turn, this means there is no one-size-fits-all policy agenda. ... The government cannot be all things to all places. It needs to decide what it is trying to achieve and how.[31]

(IFS) has stated, responding effectively to the challenge depends on recognizing the complexity both of the "left behind problem" and the "levelling up" policy resolution (Box 1.4).

For some observers, such as Newman, in the UK context, the idea of "levelling up" invokes a range of disparate political ideologies: it speaks to social democrats about tackling social deprivation, to social liberals about equality of opportunity, to economic liberals about supporting free markets, and to conservatives about reuniting the nation and a return to "One-Nation" politics.[32] He suggests that if "levelling up" develops from a political slogan into a fully fledged policy programme, it will become increasingly difficult for the government to manage the ideological tensions inherent in its "levelling-up" agenda. For other writers, "levelling up" subsumes two rather different agendas.[33] One is targeted at addressing subjective conditions of negative well-being, political discontent and dissatisfaction, and is seeking to address these rapidly by way of visible community social and public investments, which aim to help communities feel better about where they live, primarily by reducing crime and restoring local facilities and local feelings of attachment and pride. At its core, this "placemaking" agenda calls for visible investments in the public realm of high streets and town centres.[34] The second agenda, however, is much more economic and focused on a programme of longer term and more radical reduction of inter- and intra-regional differences in economic prosperity and performance, focusing on such indicators as employment, wages and productivity. While the political appeal and social value of the first agenda are certainly clear, improving the appearance and quality of local town and city centres and their street infrastructures is of itself not sufficient to deliver the second agenda of promoting long-term economic growth, and it risks being an inadequate and superficial response to a profound structural problem. We return to this issue in Chapter 5.

The notion of "levelling up" has both normative and instrumental dimensions. From a normative perspective, a guiding basic principle would argue that households should not be substantially materially worse off or disadvantaged simply by virtue of where they live. The UK Prime Minister has claimed that it is not talent that is unevenly spread across the country, but the opportunities that different areas afford to individuals (Box 1.5). Yet at the same time, the complaint is frequently made that educational attainment levels and skills tend to be low in many Northern cities and towns. This suggests a deeper problem that talent is not being fostered and nurtured in these areas. In addition, in any case, an orthodox economist would no doubt retort that if individuals feel they are disadvantaged by the lack of opportunities in their locality, then they should move to a more prosperous area where they have the opportunity to be less disadvantaged. As the resurgence of the political and policy debate about spatial inequalities and "left behind places" demonstrates, however, such reliance upon labour mobility has largely failed to materialize and ameliorate deeper seated structural problems.

Many, of course, are able and willing to make such moves. But it tends to be the younger, better-educated and more enterprising individuals who are more likely to undertake out-migration, and this merely serves to consign "left behind places" to a self-reinforcing process of falling yet further behind in talent and development, while possibly compounding upward pressure on housing, public services and resources in the more prosperous destination areas. From a normative viewpoint, there is a strong moral case for equalizing economic talent, opportunity, and welfare across regions and localities as a central part of "levelling up" and addressing the plight of "left behind places". To that end, the UK government should commit to ensuring equal per capita spending on the essential public goods and services that contribute to that aim, such as healthcare, education, transport infrastructures, and other foundational goods and services. In the short to medium terms, however, it may well be necessary for "left behind places" to receive higher per capita spending than more prosperous areas on these services and social goods in order to bring their educational attainment levels, skills, health outcomes and social infrastructures up to those in prosperous places.

But equalizing other aspects of local economic prosperity and performance such as unemployment rates or productivity, although desirable, is far more difficult. Capitalism is dynamic: change is one of its constant features; there will always be structural and other differences across regions, cities, towns and localities. Even orthodox economists recognize that the long-run equalization—convergence—of, say, regional per capita incomes or productivity is unlikely, not only because of "irreducible" differences in structural, technological and other such features between regions and localities, but also because of major shifts in those features over time, shifts that are typically uneven in their spatial impacts. Hence, economists often prefer to talk of "conditional convergence" and "club convergence" (convergence within groups of regions or areas sharing similar features, but not necessarily between different groups or clubs of regions), which imply that the degree to which places can be "levelled up" will always be conditional to some extent on such "irreducible differences", or on how far these differences themselves can in fact be reduced.

But while some degree of spatial inequality is thus inevitable, this does not detract from the need to try to minimize its scale. After all, the degree of spatial inequality in the UK (as measured by the coefficient of variation) has increased by more than 50% since the beginning of the 1980s (see Chapter 2). Economic conditions and opportunities impact on people's health and well-being. People who are better off, and have happier, more fulfilling lives and good jobs, live longer and have healthier lives than those who do not. That is the clear conclusion of decades of work on health inequalities.[36] Reducing spatial inequalities—interpreted as securing a more even distribution of productive factors and capabilities to ensure that all regions and areas have economies that, at the least, provide agreed standards of opportunity, living and welfare—should not be seen as some sort of zero-sum game.[37]

Indeed, there are strong instrumental arguments for reducing spatial inequalities, namely that it increases the utilization and productive potential of the human and business resources in "left behind places" and maximizes their contribution to national growth and development. For contrary to what many economists believe, "levelling up" need not be at the cost of national economic growth and efficiency: the so-called "equity–efficiency trade off". According to this notion, the policy choice is between faster national growth and greater social equality: one can have one or the other, but not both. Belief in this "conventional wisdom" has long permeated UK central government thinking, and especially that of the finance ministry, HM Treasury. There is in fact evidence to indicate that countries that have *lower* social inequality (as measured, say, by the Gini coefficient of per capita incomes, or some other similar index) tend to have a *higher*, not lower, rate of economic growth over the long run.

There are grounds for arguing that, similarly, countries that have a low degree of regional economic inequality likewise experience faster economic growth nationally.[38] Certainly, the empirical evidence for a downward-sloping "trade-off" between national growth and regional equality is far from unequivocal. For example, in their detailed study of regional inequality across the European Union, Gardiner et al. find no consistent evidence that greater regional balance (equality) depresses national economic growth.[39] More recent work by Capello and Cerisola suggests that disparities across regions in Europe are mainly driven by an uneven distribution of production factors rather than by the effects of spatial concentration on enhanced productivity; it is thus "not a matter of a trade-off between efficiency and [regional] cohesion, but a matter of pursuing cohesion through efficiency".[40] Securing a more spatially even distribution of productive factors—in the widest sense, from investment, to skills, to good jobs, to high-quality social, physical and soft infrastructures, to cultural amenities—would therefore not only improve the economic prosperity and performance of "left behind places" themselves, but also boost national growth.

Further, "levelling up" is not a "one-off" policy challenge, but an ongoing process that will take many years, even decades, to achieve. Just as the current problem of "left behind places" has been long in the making, so it will be long in its resolution. Benchmarks are themselves moving targets. This means that to reduce disparities in, say, average per capita income levels between cities, towns or localities, will require the *growth rates* of average per capita incomes in areas where they are well below the national average to be *higher* than in areas where average per capita incomes are above the average. This point is worth highlighting because one of the "rebalancing" aims of the New Labour government in the UK from the late 1990s to 2010 was to "equalise growth rates between the regions of the UK".[41] On the face of it, equalizing regional growth rates would seem a reasonable objective. If places that "start" with below-average levels of prosperity (e.g., per capita incomes) or performance (e.g., productivity) subsequently also have below-average growth rates, they will fall yet further behind in both relative and absolute terms. But even if growth rates were to be equalized across all regions and places, while those that "started" with below-average levels of per capita incomes or productivity would maintain their relative position, in *absolute* terms they would continue to fall further behind. This simple but obvious fact is often overlooked in those policy statements on "levelling up" or "rebalancing" that emphasize the need to bring the growth rates in "left behind regions and places" closer to those of more prosperous regions and places. To narrow spatial inequalities, in both relative and absolute terms, will in fact require such places to grow *faster* than more prosperous places, and for an extended period of time.

Finally, there is the issue of how "levelling up" is to be achieved: What are the sort of policies needed to attain that goal? So far in the UK, "levelling up" has been a highly ambiguous political objective that has gained a great deal of traction by promising to target help on discontented and marginalized communities: indeed, the phrase seems to have become the required parlance used by UK government politicians in discussions of almost any social and economic issue, typically without any detailed definition. It has generated a series of symbolic investments, restorative promises and deals, but it faces major tensions and unaddressed difficulties.[42] Nor has any time span for its achievement been specified, whereas in reality it will need to be a continuous and more-than-one-political-cycle endeavour, particularly as economic and other forces and processes themselves change over time, as the global Covid-19 pandemic has so starkly highlighted.

In the UK, as elsewhere, there have long been various policy initiatives aimed at reducing socio-economic inequalities between regions, cities and localities, in the UK's case extending back to the 1920s. In this sense, "levelling up" the economic geography of the country has been a policy aim with a long history, even if the terminology and political salience given to the notion has changed over time. However, the fact that spatial inequalities still exist after a

https://doi.org/10.1080/2578711X.2021.1992165

century of policy initiatives and experiments, and that they have widened over the past four decades or so, indicates that past policies have had limited impact. At best, they may only have prevented problems from worsening at a faster rate. And in some instances, policy has not necessarily focused on the most "left behind places"—the case of the London Docklands redevelopment being one such case. Learning from that past experience is thus an essential prerequisite for judging currently emerging policy programmes (Chapter 5) and for thinking about more strategic alternatives (Chapter 6).

Nothing short of a different model of national economic development is called for as the basis for rebuilding forward from the Covid-19 crisis, in which the pursuit of equitable regional and local growth and prosperity—"levelling up"—is not a mere adjunct to national economic policymaking, the subject of a succession of uncoordinated policy experiments and fads, *but a core foundational principle for constructing a fairer, more sustainable and more stable form of capitalism*.[43] The aim of this short book is to contribute to this objective by examining the "left behind" problem and the policy principles for resolving it. In summary, we argue for the following:

- A detailed examination of dimensions of spatial divergence and local inequality that identifies long-term economic paths and their causes, in order to move beyond simplistic binary categories such as "left behind" or "pulling ahead", or "towns versus cities", and an unhelpful overreliance on short periods of the most recent data.

- The articulation of a bold vision for economic, social and environmental development in the UK in the post-Brexit and post-pandemic context.

- The need for a more coherent and integrated approach to subnational development that better connects and coordinates institutional and policy approaches across the UK's economic geographies.

- The decentralization and devolution of appropriate powers and responsibilities to subnational institutions to enable the formulation of place-based policies that tailor institutional arrangements and policy to local contexts, problems and potentialities.

Our focus in what follows is on the experience and problems of the UK. Our justification for choosing the UK as our case study is essentially twofold. First, the UK has one of the worst levels of regional and subregional economic inequality to be found among the OECD countries. Second, at the same time it has one of the longest histories of regional and urban policies aimed at reducing those inequalities, with the first policy experiments dating from 1928. However, although the empirics and issues that follow are specific to the UK, because of these two features, there are lessons to be learned from the UK case that have potential relevance for other countries in which geographical inequalities are also attracting the attention of policymakers as they too are confronted with the challenge of "levelling up" their "left behind places".

NOTES

1 Sandbu M (2020) *The Economics of Belonging: A Radical Plan to Win Back the Left Behind and Achieve Prosperity for All*. Princeton: Princeton University Press.

2 For example, Moretti E (2012) *The New Geography of Jobs*. Boston: Mariner; Organisation for Economic Co-operation and Development (OECD) (2016) *Regional Outlook: Productive Regions for Inclusive Societies*. Paris: OECD; Hendrikson C and Muro M (2020) *Will COVID-19 Rebalance America's Uneven Economic Geography? Don't Bet On It* (Brookings Metro's COVID-19 Analysis). Washington, DC: Brookings Institution; Rosés JR and Wolf N (2019) *The Economic Development of Europe's Regions: A Quantitative History Since 1900*. London: Routledge; Rosés JR and Wolf N (2021) Regional inequality in the long-run, Europe 1900–2015. *Oxford Review of Economic Policy*, 37: 17–48; Iammarino S, Rodríguez-Pose A and Storper M (2019) Regional inequality in Europe: Evidence, theory and policy. *Journal of Economic Geography*, 17: 273–298; Odendahl C, Springford J, Johnson S and Murray J (2019) *The Big Sort? The Diverging Fortunes of Europe's Regions*. London: Centre for European Reform.

3 Moretti (2012), p. 26, see Reference 2.

4 Rosés and Wolf (2021), pp. 35–36, see Reference 2.

5 Ulrich-Schad J and Duncan C (2018) People and places left behind: Work, culture and politics in the rural United States. *Journal of Peasant Studies* 45(1): 59–79; Lichter DT and Schafft KA (2016) People and places left behind: Rural poverty in the new century. In D Brady and L Burton (eds.), *The Oxford Handbook of the Social Science of Poverty*, pp. 317–339. Oxford: Oxford University Press; Fan C and Chen C (2020) Left behind? Migration stories of two women in rural China. *Social Inclusion*, 8: 47–57.

6 World Bank (2009) *Reshaping Economic Geography*. Washington, DC: World Bank.

7 Moretti (2012), see Reference 2.

8 Hendrickson C, Muro M and Galston WA (2018) *Countering the Geography of Discontent: Strategies for Left Behind Places*, p. 4. Washington, DC: Brookings Institution.

9 Storper M (2018) Separate worlds: Explaining the current wave of regional economic polarization. *Journal of Economic Geography*, 18: 247–270.

10 Rosés and Wolf (2021), see Reference 2.

11 Odendahl et al. (2020); and Rosés and Wolf (2021), see Reference 2.

12 Martin RL, Pike A, Tyler P and Gardiner B. (2015) *Spatially Rebalancing the UK Economy: The Need for a New Policy Model*. London: Regional Studies Association; McCann P (2016) *The UK Regional–National Economic Problem: Geography, Globalisation and Governance*. London: Routledge; Agrawal S and Phillips D (2020) *Catching Up or Falling Behind? Geographical Inequalities in the UK and How they Have Changed in Recent Years*. London: Institute for Fiscal Studies; UK2070 Commission, 2020 (2019) *Fairer and Stronger: Rebalancing the UK Economy*. London: UK2070.

13 Deutsche Bank (2013) *London and the UK Economy: In for a Penny, In for a Pound?* London: Deutsche Bank Markets Research; Tyler P, Evenhuis E, Martin RL, Sunley P and Gardiner B (2017). Growing apart? Structural transformation and the uneven development of British cities. *Cambridge Journal of Regions, Economy and Society*, 10: 425–454; McCann (2016), see Reference 12.

14 Martin RL (2006) The contemporary debate over the North–South divide: Images and realities of regional inequality in late-twentieth century Britain. In ARH Baker and M Billinge (eds.), *Geographies of*

England: The North–South Divide, Imagined and Material, pp. 15–43. Cambridge: Cambridge University Press; Geary F and Stark T (2015) Regional GDP in the UK, 1861–1911: New estimates. *Economic History Review*, 68: 123–144; Geary F and Stark T (2016) What happened to regional inequality in Britain in the twentieth century? *Economic History Review*, 69: 215–228; see also Chapter 2 below.

[15] Martin et al. (2015), see Reference 12.

[16] Hendrikson et al. (2018), see Reference 8; Dijkstra L, Poelman H and Rodríguez-Pose A (2020) *The Geography of EU Discontent* (Working Paper No. 12/2018). Brussels: European Commission; De Ruyter A, Martin RL and Tyler P (2021) The geographies of discontent: Sources, manifestations and consequences. *Cambridge Journal of Regions, Economy and Society*, 14: 381–393; Cambridge Journal of Regions, Economy and Society (2021) Special issue: The Geographies of discontent: causes, manifestations and consequences, *Cambridge Journal of Regions, Economy and Society*, 14(3): 381–642.

[17] Rodríguez-Pose A (2018). The revenge of places that don't matter (and what to do about it). *Cambridge Journal of Regions, Economy and Society*, 11: 189–209.

[18] Donald Trump, Presidential Campaign Speech on Jobs and the Economy, 15 September 2016. https://time.com/4495507/donald-trump-economy-speech-transcript/

[19] Muro M, Byerly-Duke A, You Y and Maxim R (2020) *Biden-Voting Counties Equal 70% of America's Economy*. Washington, DC: Brookings Institution. https://www.brookings.edu/blog/the-avenue/2020/11/09/biden-voting-counties-equal-70-of-americas-economy-what-does-this-mean-for-the-nations-political-economic-divide/.

[20] Jennings W and Stoker G (2016) The bifurcation of politics: Two Englands. *Political Quarterly*, 87: 372–382.

[21] See https://www.gov.uk/government/publications/the-ten-point-plan-for-a-green-industrial-revolution/.

[22] See https://ww.gov.ukgovernment/publications/national-infrastructure-strategy/.

[23] Prime Minister Boris Johnson, Speech on New Deal for Britain, 30 June 2020. https://www.gov.uk/government/speeches/pm-economy-speech-30-june-2020

[24] Prime Minister Boris Johnson, Build Back Better: Our Plan for Growth, 3 March 2021, at 7. https://www.gov.uk/government/publications/build-back-better-our-plan-for-growth/build-back-better-our-plan-for-growth-html

[25] See https://assets.publishing.service.gov.uk/government/uploads/system/uploads/attachment_data/file/853811/IoD2019_FAQ_v4.pdf/.

[26] Davenport and Zaranko (2020) *Levelling Up: Where and How*. London: Institute for Fiscal Studies.

[27] Local Trust (2020) *Left Behind Neighbourhoods*. https://localtrust.org.uk/policy/left-behind-neighbourhoods/.

[28] Bolton M, Day R and Leach M (2020) England's overlooked neighbourhoods: Defining, understanding and regenerating 'left behind' communities. *Journal of Urban Regeneration and Renewal*, 12: 116–123.

[29] Boswell J, Denham J, Furlong J, Killick A, Ndugga P, Rek B, Ryan M and Shipp J (2020) Place-based politics and nested deprivation in the U.K.: Beyond cities–towns, 'Two Englands' and the 'Left Behind'. *Representation*. 10.1080/00344893.2020.1751258.

[30] Tomaney T and Pike A (2020) Levelling up? *Political Quarterly*, 91: 43–48.

[31] Davenport and Zaranko (2020), ch. 7, pp. 1–2, see Reference 26.

[32] Newman J (2021) The ambiguous ideology of levelling up. *Political Quarterly*, 92: 312–320.

[33] Jennings W, McKay L and Stoker G (2021) The politics of levelling up. *Political Quarterly*, 92: 302–311.

[34] Wolf R (2021) Tests for the delivery of levelling up, and levers with which to deliver it. *Conservative Home*, 10 May. https://www.conservativehome.com/platform/2021/05/rachel-wolf-tests-for-the-delivery-of-levelling-up-and-levers-with-which-deliver-it.html/.

[35] Prime Minister Boris Johnson, The Prime Minister's Levelling Up Speech, 15 July 2021. https://www.gov.uk/government/speeches/the-prime-ministers-levelling-up-speech-15-july-2021/.

[36] Marmot M, Allen J, Boyce T, Goldblatt P and Morrison J (2020) *Health Equity in England: The Marmot Review 10 Years On*. London: Institute of Health Equity.

[37] When talk of "rebalancing" the British economy began to gain traction following the financial crisis, policy and business leaders in London were quick to warn that "levelling up" the country "could damage the capital's status as a world-leading city". This response not only seemed to subscribe to the misguided belief that pursuing a more equitable geographical distribution of economic success and prosperity would necessarily be at the expense of London, and national efficiency in general, but also smacked precisely of the elitist detachment that has fuelled social and political discontent in the British regions. For example, see *Financial Times* (2010) London's leaders warn over push to narrow regional inequalities. *Financial Times*, 13 January. https://www.ft.com/content/ad1bc24e-339d-11ea-9703-eea0cae3f0de/.

[38] Evenhuis E, Lee N, Martin RL and Tyler P (2021) Rethinking the political economy of place: Challenges of productivity and inclusion. *Cambridge Journal of Regions, Economy and Society*, 14: 3–14.

[39] Gardiner B, Martin R and Tyler P (2011) Does spatial agglomeration increase national growth? Evidence from the European Union. *Journal of Economic Geography*, 11: 979–1006.

[40] Capello R and Cerisola S (2020) Concentrated versus diffused growth assets: Agglomeration economies and regional cohesion. *Growth and Change*, 51: 1440–1453, at 1449.

[41] This was the explicit aim as set out in the then government's Public Service Agreement 8; HM Treasury, Department of Trade and Industry, and Office of the Deputy Prime Minister (2003) *A Modern Regional Policy for the United Kingdom*. London: HMSO.

[42] Jennings et al. (2021), see Reference 33.

[43] Collier P (2018) *The Future of Capitalism: Facing the New Anxieties*. London: Allen Lane.

2. BECOMING "LEFT BEHIND": HOW PLACES HAVE GROWN APART

Keywords: left behind problem, great turnaround, falling behind, regional divergence, productivity puzzle

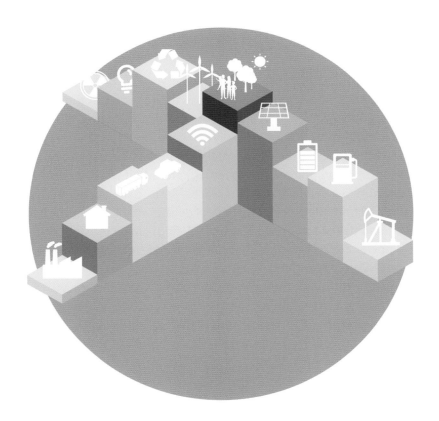

2.1 SITUATING THE "LEFT BEHIND" PROBLEM

Places—regions, cities, towns and local communities—can get "left behind" economically and socially for a whole variety of reasons.[2] Shifts in international competition, loss of exports, changes in domestic consumer demand, major technological developments or substantial changes in economic policy may all undermine or render obsolete certain of a place's industries, firms and local labour skills.

Standing at the pinnacle of the present and looking back, it is clear that the late 1970s to early 1980s marked one such "hinge of history" in the development of the advanced industrialized nations, a shift that can be broadly described as being from a post-war "Keynesian-welfare state"-type model of economic development to more a more market-oriented' and "neoliberal–globalist" model. To be sure, both "models" had different variants across different advanced economies (the "varieties of capitalism argument"), but as Streeck has stressed,[3] longitudinal commonalities in the nature of the shift between growth regimes—commonalities in the "direction of travel"—have been more important than differences in the precise details of each nation's version of the two models.

The progress of this major shift in growth regime since the beginning of the 1980s—what is frequently referred to as an economic and cultural transition to "post-industrialism"—has had profound implications socially and spatially. Its creative and destructive effects have not been economically, socially or spatially neutral. Geographically, not all regions, cities, towns and local communities have been able to adapt equally successfully to the changes and opportunities involved. Certain places—especially those less burdened by the structures inherited from the preceding phase of development, those which have spearheaded the new technologies of our age, or those in which the main levers of economic, financial and political power are concentrated—have led the new growth regime, whilst many other places more burdened and less adaptable have struggled to achieve a similar growth momentum and prosperity. The upshot has been a major new phase of geographically divergent development. It is in terms of this historic systemic transformation that today's problem of "left behind places", in the UK and elsewhere, needs to be situated and explained, and the immense scale of the policy challenge to "level up" those places must be appreciated. We take up this issue in Chapter 3.

Regional Studies Policy Impact Books

https://doi.org/10.1080/2578711X.2021.1992168

2.2 THE "GREAT TURNAROUND": FROM CONVERGENCE TO DIVERGENCE

In the United States, for example, while inequalities in per capita incomes at both the state level and between metropolitan areas had been narrowing between the 1950s and 1970s, they began to widen from the 1980s onwards (Figure 2.1). In the UK, a similar turnaround from convergence to divergence occurred in per capita output across both the 12 broad standard regions and the 370 local authority districts (LADs) (Figure 2.2). In Europe, too, the 1980s marked a turning point between convergence and divergence.[4] This geographical differentiation reveals a sharpening pattern of spatial inequality.

Some authors attribute this shift almost entirely to the impact of the technological changes that have unfolded over the past 40 years, and especially to the implications of digitization and innovation.[5] Although Sandbu also considers technological change to have been a key cause of the widening of spatial inequalities in the United States and across Europe, he points the major finger of blame at Western governments' abandonment of the post-war Keynesian and welfarist macroeconomic policy consensus, and what he argues has since been "half a century of policy mistakes".[6]

Figure 2.1   From convergence to divergence: coefficient of variation of per capita personal incomes across US states (1960–2019) and metro areas (1969–2019)

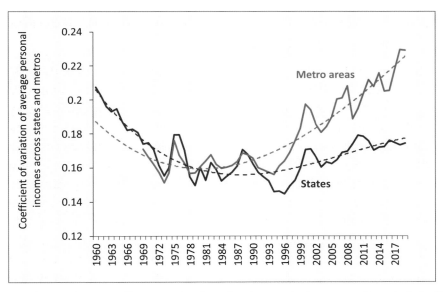

Note: Data are real per capita personal incomes, using the national personal price consumption price index (2012 prices) as the deflator. States exclude Alaska and Hawaii. Data for 384 metropolitan statistical areas are only available from 1969 onwards. Trend lines are fitted fourth-order polynomials.
Source: Authors' own elaboration using data from the US Bureau of Economic Analysis.

While Sandbu largely absolves globalization from any significant culpability, arguing that it has been unfairly "scapegoated" by many commentators,[7] Rodrik argues that globalization—or what he calls "hyper-globalisation"—cannot be exonerated quite so easily.[8] In his view, the untrammelled pursuit of hyper-globalization by governments, financial institutions, and technological and corporate elites alike has made it difficult to achieve social and regional inclusion at home.

2.3 GROWING APART: MACRO-GEOGRAPHIES OF "FALLING BEHIND"

What is apparent in Figures 2.1 and 2.2 is that spatial divergence is even evident at broad geographical scales. In fact, in the UK, much of the recurring debate over geographical socio-economic inequality has been focused at a particularly broad level, on what in the 1980s became labelled as a "North–South divide", the growing gap between a more prosperous and dynamic "South", on the one hand, and the "rest" of the country, the "North", on the other.[9]

Since the early 1980s, however, the divide has widened appreciably, to a degree greater than at any other time over the past century or more (Table 2.1).

Figure 2.2   From convergence to divergence: coefficient of variation of gross value added per capita across UK standard regions and local authority districts, 1971–2018

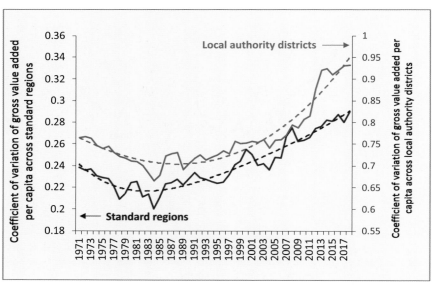

Note: Gross value added is in national 2016 prices: local price deflators are not available. Trend lines are fitted fourth-order polynomials. See note 17 for the use of local authority districts.
Source: Authors' own elaboration using data from Cambridge Econometrics.

Table 2.1 Long-run regional inequalities in Britain: gross domestic product (GDP) per capita, relative to the national average, 1901–2018

	1901	1911	1921	1931	1938	1951	1961	1971	1981	1991	1998	2001	2011	2018
London	134.2	133.8	137.4	144.2	147.1	138.6	145.3	153.3	163.7	165.6	164.5	169.6	172.9	177.4
South East	107.0	104.1	101.2	112.5	102.9	84.8	88.1	105.7	104.3	107.1	113.7	113.18	110.7	106.6
East of England	83.7	83.5	83.5	88.9	86.7	89.0	92.4	103.8	100.1	97.4	96.9	97.2	90.2	93.2
South West	91.7	92.4	91.3	92.3	89.7	89.3	88.9	90.9	94.1	92.0	91.2	91.9	90.2	87.4
East Midlands	92.4	97.2	88.6	86.6	89.3	95.8	94.7	80.7	85.0	84.7	87.6	85.1	82.3	79.6
West Midlands	86.0	90.5	88.6	95.7	96.6	104.0	104.0	96.4	89.8	90.0	88.9	86.7	81.8	84.1
Yorkshire and Humberside	88.3	90.1	93.6	86.4	88.0	97.5	94.1	80.7	85.5	84.7	83.7	82.9	81.6	79.2
North West	103.7	104.8	109.3	86.1	93.1	104.0	95.9	93.9	85.8	85.0	85.9	87.2	87.4	88.2
North East	85.8	83.0	83.1	65.0	76.4	88.6	89.6	75.3	79.2	75.8	74.6	72.9	71.7	72.1
Wales	80.3	82.1	76.5	81.1	76.1	84.9	90.7	78.5	78.2	75.3	75.0	73.3	73.7	72.8
Scotland	90.5	86.9	92.3	94.2	93.9	89.3	89.0	92.2	97.8	96.1	91.3	90.3	94.2	91.7
Northern Ireland	–	–	–	–	–	–		80.1	84.6	77.8	78.7	82.3	77.0	78.7
Coefficient of variation	16.9	16.6	18.5	22.6	17.5	18.8	17.6	19.1	22.9	23.8	25.9	27.5	29.4	30.6

Note: Data for 1901–61 are from Geary and Stark[10] and refer to Great Britain (data for Northern Ireland being unavailable). Data for 1971–91 are from the UK Regional Data Base complied by Cambridge Econometrics. Data for 1998–2018 are from Office for National Statistics (ONS). The regional boundaries used by Geary and Stark differ in some respects from those used for 1971 onwards. Thus, there are some unavoidable discontinuities across the entire data series, although the scale of those discontinuities is unlikely to have dramatically altered the main trends shown. GDP is workplace based, and thus makes no allowance for workers commuting across regional boundaries.

Using 1981 as a base year, by 2018 the "South" had opened up a cumulative differential growth gap of some 20 percentage points over the "North" (Figure 2.3), and a cumulative differential employment growth gap of 19 percentage points (Figure 2.4).[11] The notion of cumulative differential growth was used by Blanchard and Katz,[12] in their seminal study of regional economic evolutions in the United States, to show how individual states had diverged in terms of employment growth over the post-war period, using the US average as the reference series. Given that London is often singled out as the "exemplar" or "reference benchmark" against which other UK regions and cities are compared in policy discourses, it is important to note how until the early 1990s London actually behaved more like the country's "North". Over the 1970s and 1980s, like many Northern cities and towns, London experienced the rapid deindustrialization of its manufacturing base (see Chapter 3).[13]

But the competitive benefits unleashed by Margaret Thatcher's government's deregulation of the UK's financial and banking system in 1986—the so-called "Big Bang"—subsequently gave London, as the national financial hub, a major opportunity to "reinvent" its economy as a leading global financial centre.[14] This surge of finance-driven growth was only temporarily interrupted by the global financial crisis of 2007–08, owing in large part to the government's massive bailing out of the major banks and financial institutions and partial and wholesale nationalizations. Indeed, what is so striking is just how powerfully London recovered from

Figure 2.3 Cumulative percentage point differential output growth, Southern and Northern Britain, 1981–2018

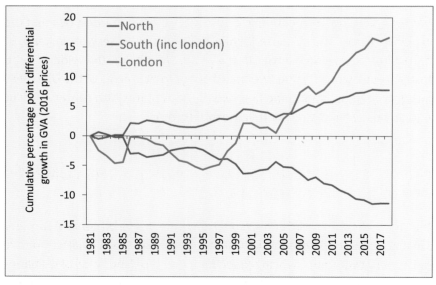

Note: Gross value added (GVA) is in 2016 prices; the cumulative differential is from the Great Britain growth rate.
Source: Authors' own elaboration using data from Cambridge Econometrics.

https://doi.org/10.1080/2578711X.2021.1992168

Figure 2.4 Cumulative percentage point differential employment growth, Southern and Northern Britain, 1981–2018

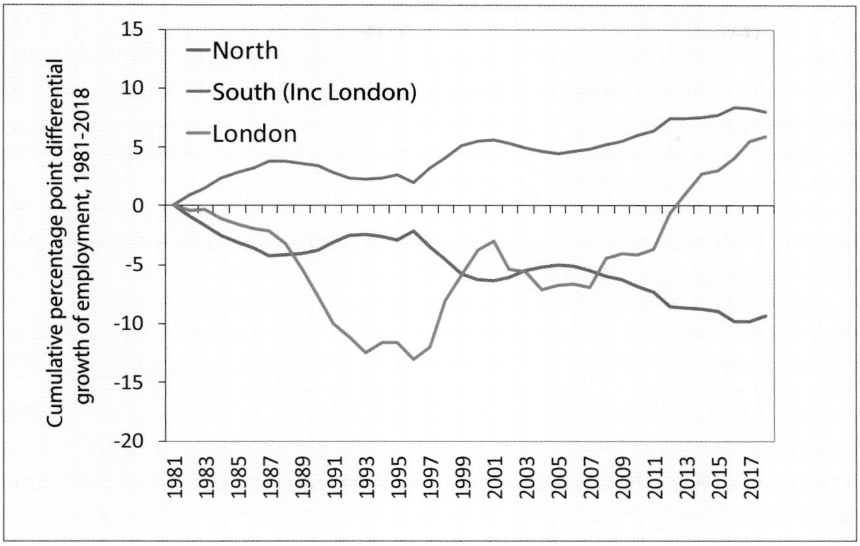

Note: The cumulative differential is from the Great Britain growth rate. Recessionary downturns in employment last longer than for output.
Source: Authors' own elaboration using data from Cambridge Econometrics.

the global financial crisis-induced recession of 2008–10, in the growth both of its output and its employment.

Some observers had argued in the late 1990s that the "North–South divide" had ceased to be a prominent feature of the UK's economic landscape.[15] The assumption was that the deindustrialization of the "North", and its consequential dependence on services instead as the driver of growth, had in effect removed the source of the "North–South divide". That prediction has manifestly proved wrong: these two broad geographical areas of the UK have continued to pull apart economically during the first two decades of the 20th century. The question of spatial inequality has endured rather than been resolved.

2.4 FROM BROAD REGIONS TO LOCAL PLACES: THE COMPLEXITY OF THE "LEFT BEHIND" LANDSCAPE

But both the "North–South divide" and regional disparities in the UK conceal considerable local variations in economic conditions, performance and prosperity. This pattern was recognized by the New Labour government, which argued for an "archipelago" view of spatial inequalities, rather than one of a major fault line between a lagging "North" and a leading "South" (Box 2.1). Few would disagree with this argument: to a significant extent, the "North–South divide" is itself a metaphor, a discursive device for simplifying what is necessarily a complex and evolving socio-economic landscape.

As one way of capturing this local picture, if we focus on the 370 LADs that span Britain, the heterogeneity of local growth gaps since the beginning of the 1980s becomes evident.[17] Figure 2.5 plots the cumulative differential annual growth of output (gross value added— GVA) against that of employment for each LAD over the period 1981–2018. The corresponding geographies, by quartiles, of cumulative differential employment and output growth for the 370 LADs over 1981–2018 are shown in Figure 2.6.

Figure 2.5   Relationship between cumulative differential growth gaps for output and employment, 370 local authority districts (LADs), 1981–2018

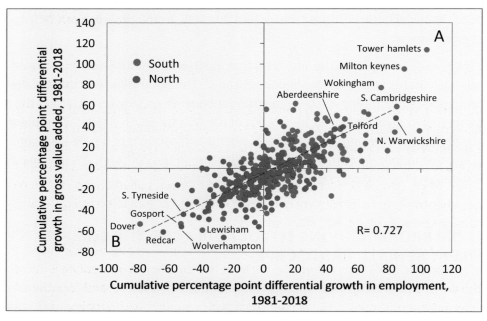

Note: South refers to LADs in the Southern regions; North refers to LADs in Northern regions (for definitions of Northern and Southern regions, see note 9). This geographical classification of LADs is used throughout in subsequent discussions and chapters.
Source: Authors' own elaboration using data from Cambridge Econometrics.

https://doi.org/10.1080/2578711X.2021.1992168

Figure 2.6   Local geographies of cumulative percentage point differential employment and output growth, 1981–2018

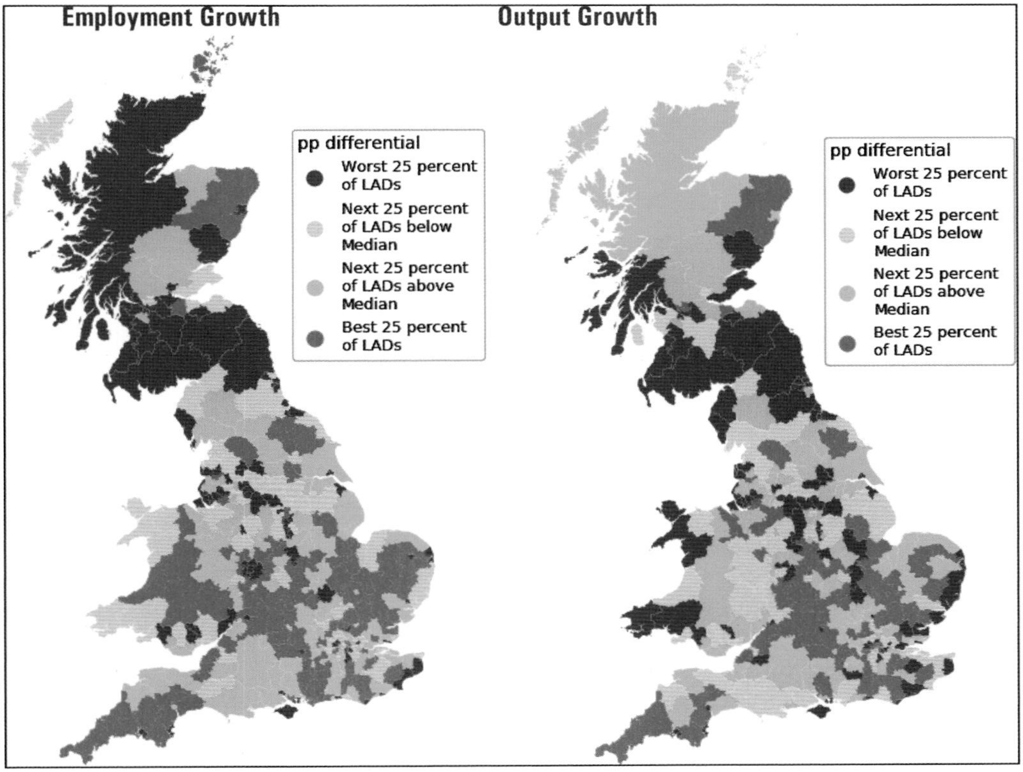

Note: There were a total of 370 local authority districts (LADs) by quartiles.

Overall, there is a moderately strong positive association between differential output growth and differential employment growth ($R=0.727$): localities that have grown faster than the British economy as a whole in terms of output have also tended to grow faster in employment. The larger a locality's positive growth gaps for both employment and output (top right-hand quadrant A of Figure 2.5), the more it might be said to have "pulled ahead" of the national average, while the larger a locality's negative growth gaps (bottom left-hand quadrant B), the more it might be argued to have "fallen behind".

But what is striking is the variability of the patchwork geography of local performance (Figure 2.6), with several top performing LADs (in the top 25%) in immediate juxtaposition with the worst performing (bottom 25%). Further, both "Northern" and "Southern" LADs can be found in both groups. Nevertheless, it is the case that with employment, and to a lesser extent output, the largest number of best performing localities are concentrated in the Southern half of Britain. This is certainly apparent if we consider the worst 25% of LADs in terms of *both* employment and output growth (some 74 such localities), listed in Table 2.2.

https://doi.org/10.1080/2578711X.2021.1992168

https://doi.org/10.1080/2578711X.2021.1992168

Table 2.2 The 74 "Left behind" local authority districts, defined as in the bottom quartile of cumulative differential growth of both employment and output (cumulative annual percentage point difference from national growth), 1981–2018:

Locality	Employment growth	GVA growth	Settlement type	Broad region	Locality	Employment growth	GVA growth	Settlement type	Broad region
Dover	−79.15	−53.32	Medium town	South	Walsall	−23.07	−20.23	Medium town	North
Redcar and Cleveland	−64.30	−60.83	Medium town	North	Ealing	−22.58	−21.17	London	South
Clackmannanshire	−55.05	−15.92	Small town	North	Oadby and Wigston	−22.51	−13.06	Medium town	South
Gosport	−53.09	−52.96	Large town	South	Southampton	−22.50	−14.97	Other city	South
Wolverhampton	−52.58	−55.63	Other city	North	Sheffield	−22.37	−25.63	Core city	North
South Tyneside	−51.42	−43.79	Large town	North	Sefton	−21.63	−26.73	Medium town	North
Inverclyde	−48.61	−34.24	Medium town	North	Shetland Islands	−20.95	−13.80	Village/rural	North
Torfaen	−45.94	−21.01	Medium town	North	Angus	−20.23	−24.48	Small town	North
Neath Port Talbot	−45.43	−44.33	Medium town	North	Hastings	−18.84	−20.38	Large town	South
Hartlepool	−43.24	−32.00	Large town	North	Glasgow City	−18.27	−22.47	Core city	North
West Dunbartonshire	−41.38	−46.89	Village/rural	North	Broxtowe	−18.18	−40.38	Medium town	South
Lewisham	−39.43	−58.96	London	South	Barrow-in-Furness	−18.18	−14.46	Medium town	North
Liverpool	−37.52	−41.41	Core city	North	Dudley	−17.93	−12.59	Medium town	North
Dundee City	−35.57	−37.08	Large town	North	Plymouth	−17.52	−22.70	Other city	South
Portsmouth	−35.42	−40.60	Other city	South	South Lanarkshire	−17.41	−17.54	Medium town	North
St Helens	−35.27	−48.76	Large town	North	Renfrewshire	−16.55	−11.09	Large town	North
Kingston upon Hull	−34.84	−33.40	Other city	North	Eastbourne	−16.16	−27.42	Large town	South
Blaenau Gwent	−34.39	−20.49	Small town	North	Bedford	−15.89	−28.07	Large town	South
Croydon	−34.23	−33.13	London	South	Bradford	−15.49	−15.48	Other city	North

District	Value	Settlement type	Region	District	Value	Settlement type	Region
Middlesbrough	−32.21	Other city	North	Chesterfield	−15.24	Large town	South
Tameside	−32.05	Medium town	North	Folkestone and Hythe	−14.91	Medium town	South
Leicester	−30.65	Other city	South	Knowsley	−14.75	Core city	North
Birmingham	−28.05	Core city	North	High Peak	−13.90	Village/rural	South
North East Lincolnshire	−27.18	Large town	North	Southend-on-Sea	−13.88	Other city	South
Blackpool	−27.07	Large town	North	Torbay	−13.83	Large town	South
Norwich	−26.79	Other city	South	Caerphilly	−12.32	Small town	North
Great Yarmouth	−26.38	Medium town	South	Northumberland	−12.01	Village/rural	North
Midlothian	−26.09	Small town	North	Newcastle on Tyne	−12.00	Core city	North
South Ayrshire	−25.99	Medium town	North	Dumfries and Galloway	−11.79	Village/rural	North
Copeland	−25.79	Village/rural	North	Isle of Wight	−11.79	Small town	South
Fylde	−25.54	Medium town	North	Adur	−11.65	Medium town	South
East Ayrshire	−25.48	Village/rural	North	Ashfield	−11.47	Medium town	South
Oldham	−25.15	Large town	North	Brent	−11.38	London	South
Wirral	−25.10	Large town	North	Argyll and Bute	−11.16	Village/rural	North
Barking and Dagenham	−24.58	London	South	Rochdale	−11.15	Large town	North
North Lanarkshire	−23.48	Medium town	North	Wigan	−10.92	Small town	North
Charnwood	−23.30	Large town	South	Scottish Borders	−10.29	Village/rural	North

Note: See also Figure 2.5. Districts are classified into settlement types and by "North" and "South".

https://doi.org/10.1080/2578711X.2021.1992168

What is also apparent in Table 2.2 is the varied geography of the types of places that have lagged behind, ranging from small towns, to medium and large towns, to small cities, to some of the UK's major cities, including the so-called "core cities" of Liverpool, Birmingham, Glasgow and Sheffield. (Figures 2.7 and 2.8). With respect to London, while as a whole it has enjoyed a remarkable success over recent decades, closer examination reveals that this has been primarily due to the employment and especially output growth performance of just a few of its boroughs, including Tower Hamlets, Islington, Hackney, Camden, Southwark and Hounslow. Indeed, on employment, the borough districts of Lewisham, Croydon, Barking and Dagenham, and Ealing have all grown much slower than the national average; while on output nearly a quarter of the boroughs (including the four just mentioned) have cumulative differential growth gaps of more than 20 percentage points below the national average. The pattern of output growth, especially, shows how London is in fact a "city of two halves". Any argument that London is proof that "agglomeration breeds success" is thus far too simplistic.

In the United States, the increasing disparity in cumulative growth across the urban system has attracted considerable discussion.[18] Attention has focused on how, at one extreme, a club of winning "super cities", "brain hubs" and "star cities"—such as San Francisco, Boston, Durham, San Jose, New York and Washington, DC—have pulled away in terms of employment and wage growth, while at the other extreme, former industrial cities and those stuck with the "wrong" industries and a limited human capital base—such as Columbus, Binghampton,

Figure 2.7   Divided London: cumulative differential employment growth gaps (percentage points) across London borough districts

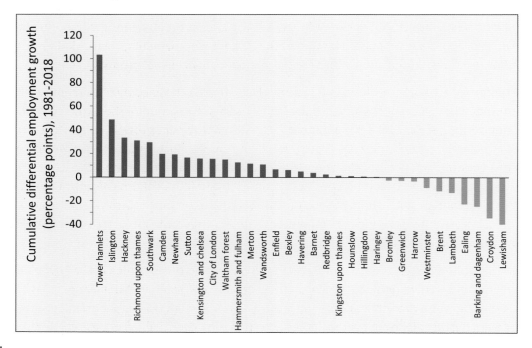

https://doi.org/10.1080/2578711X.2021.1992168

Figure 2.8   Divided London: cumulative differential output (gross value added—GVA) growth gaps (percentage points) across London borough districts

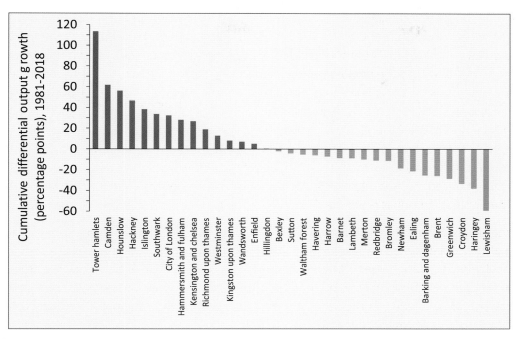

Flint and Jackson—have managed only slow and sluggish growth and form a "losing (or "left behind") club" (Figures 2.9 and 2.10). This divergence has been especially marked since the 2008 global financial crisis. For example, the 53 very largest metros (those with populations of over 1 million), have accounted for 72% of the nation's employment growth. Medium-sized cities have followed them, while the smallest metro areas have lost ground.[19]

The pattern of economic evolutions across the UK's 370 LADs classified by settlement type has been somewhat different from that of the United States. The group of the large "core cities" has not performed well in terms of output (GVA) or employment growth, being the slowest growing of any of the settlement types (Figures 2.11 and 2.12), falling progressively behind not just London, but all other city and town groups. While the large urban concentrations of economic activity and growth retain their important absolute economic weight in the UK's economic geography, it is the smaller places that have grown more quickly. This varied geographical experience has important implications for the "city centrism" of much spatial policy in the UK in recent years.[20]

As in the United States, the geography of wage growth across localities in the UK has also been uneven and divergent. But again, unlike in the United States, in the UK large cities have not been the wage growth leaders (Figure 2.13), and only London has progressively pulled away from the rest of the country, including the core cities, especially after the mid-1980s.[21] In

Figure 2.9   Divergent employment growth across US cities, 1969–2016 (indexed at 1969 = 100)

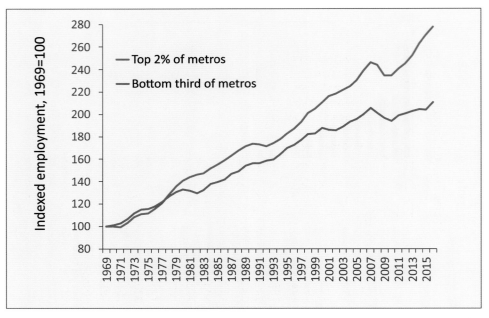

Source: Authors using data kindly supplied by Marc Muro of the Brookings Institution, Washington, DC, and referring to 350 metropolitan statistical areas.

Figure 2.10   Divergent real wage growth across US cities, 1969–2016 (indexed at 1969 = 100)

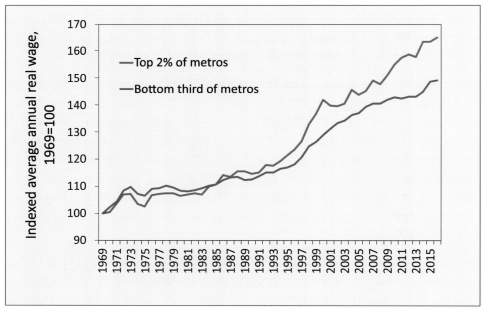

Note: See Figure 2.6.

Figure 2.11   Divergent employment growth across UK cities and towns, 1981–2018 (indexed at 1981 = 100)

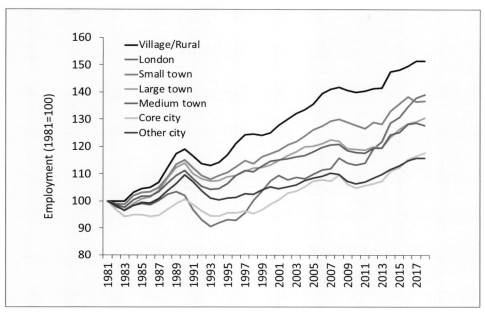

Source: Authors' own elaboration using data from Cambridge Econometrics.

Figure 2.12   Divergent real output growth (gross value added (GVA) in £ 2016) across UK cities and towns, 1981–2018 (indexed at 1981 = 100)

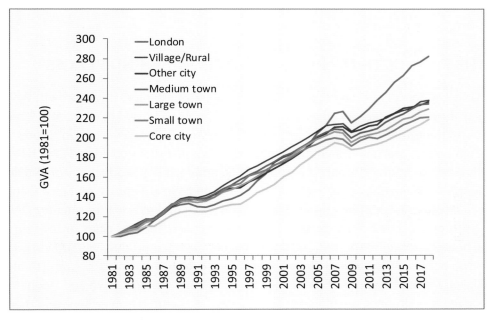

Note: Constructed from data from Cambridge Econometrics.

Figure 2.13   Divergent real wage growth (in £ 2016) across British cities and towns, 1981–2018 (indexed at 1981 = 100)

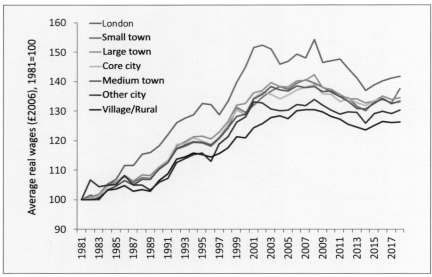

Source: Authors' own elaboration using data from Cambridge Econometrics.

all cases, the global financial crisis brought real wage growth to a halt, and for some years real wages fell, including in London, and only recently have they begun to grow again. Such real wage declines and resulting falls in living standards have been seen as important contributors to the discontent expressed in the UK and elsewhere in the last decade (see Chapter 1).

2.5 THE PRODUCTIVITY PUZZLE AND "LEFT BEHIND PLACES"

In the UK, a key policy issue has been the slowdown in the rate of productivity growth. Reviving productivity growth is seen by government and many observers as a key element of "levelling up". For example, according to the Centre for Progressive Policy, "levelling up" productivity in the "left behind" parts of Britain, and especially Northern Britain, could add £242 billion (or 13%) annually to national output.[22] Like output and employment, productivity growth across the country has been divergent, especially since the mid-1980s (Figure 2.14). Since then, productivity advance in London has pulled away from much of the rest of the country. Only the other city group of localities has come close to keeping pace. The core cities, once again, have lagged behind: between 1981 and 2018, a 20 percentage point productivity growth gap had opened up between London and the core city group. Large towns, small towns and rural areas have likewise fallen behind. As Figure 2.14 shows, the marked slowdown and stagnation of productivity growth since the global financial crisis has occurred everywhere, and there are as yet few signs of a major recovery.

   https://doi.org/10.1080/2578711X.2021.1992168

Figure 2.14   Divergent labour productivity growth (gross value added per employed person, in £ 2016) across UK cities and towns, 1981–2018 (indexed at 1971= 100)

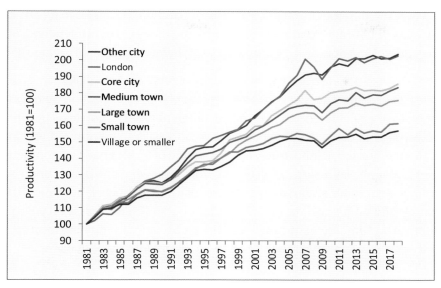

Note: Constructed from data from Cambridge Econometrics.

Comparing local productivity levels in 1971 with those in 2018 is revealing (Figure 2.15). Most "Northern" LADs had below-average productivity in 1981. While some of these had managed to raise their productivity levels above the national average by 2018, the majority still had

Figure 2.15   Local productivity levels (370 local authority districts—LADs), 1981 and 2018

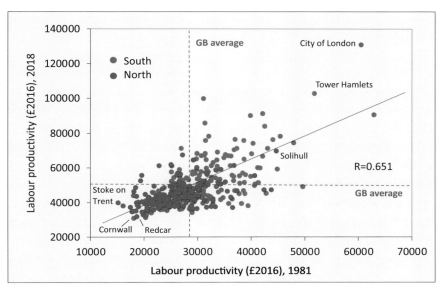

Source: Authors' own elaboration using data from Cambridge Econometrics.

below-average productivity in 2018. And a significant number of "Southern" localities are also to be found in this "remained behind" group. What is equally noteworthy is the highly varied experience over the past four decades of the many "Southern" localities that had above-average productivity in 1981: although some have increased their lead over this period, others have actually lost ground and now have productivity levels below the national average (Figure 2.16).

There is considerable debate over why productivity differs so substantially across the regions, cities and localities. Differences in economic structure and specialization go only some way in accounting for these differences.[23] The mix of different types of firm (e.g., by function, age, ownership, vintage of capital), differences in access to skills, in investment and innovation, in export orientation, and in infrastructure—in a range of local capacities, competences and externalities—may all play a part. In fact, it is far from clear what one is measuring in attempting to compare aggregate productivity between places.[24] As such, labour productivity may not be that helpful on its own for identifying "left behind" places, as it may disguise quite different output and employment dynamics from area to area. Comparing local employment growth with local productivity growth gives some insight into these dynamics.[25]

Figure 2.16   Labour productivity (gross value added (GVA) per employed person), 2018

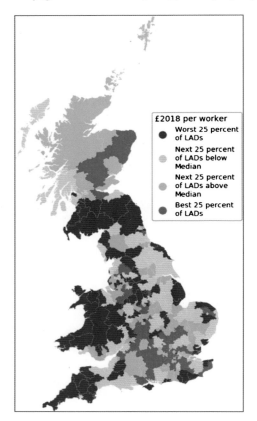

Figure 2.17 plots cumulative differential labour productivity growth against cumulative differential employment for the 370 LADs over the period 1981–2018. While most "Northern" localities have had negative differential employment growth over the period, many of these have managed to achieve positive differential productivity growth, a process we might term "productivity-biased restructuring". In contrast, whilst many "Southern" localities have experienced positive differential employment growth, many of these have recorded negative differential productivity growth, a process we might correspondingly call "employment-biased restructuring", possibly suggesting that much of the job growth in these places has been in activities with limited scope for productivity advance. It appears that relatively few localities

Figure 2.17 Local cumulative differential productivity growth and employment growth (370s local authority districts—LADs), 1981–2018

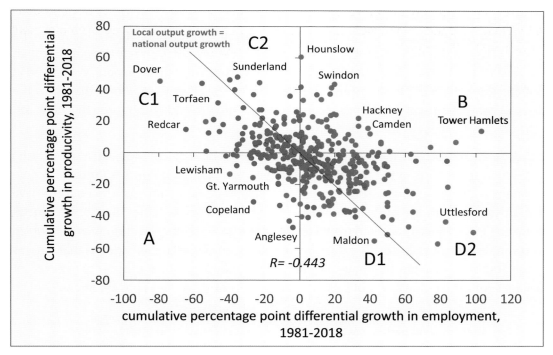

Note: Red = Southern LADs; and blue = Northern LADs.
A, vicious circle: LADs with productivity, employment and output growth all below the national average
B, virtuous circle: LADs with productivity, employment and output growth all above the national average
C1, restructuring towards productivity: LADs with productivity growth above the national average, but employment and output growth both below the national average
C2, restructuring towards productivity: LADs with productivity growth and output growth above the national average, but employment growth below the national average
D1, restructuring towards employment: LADs with employment growth above the national average, but productivity growth and output growth both below the national average
D2, restructuring towards employment: LADs with employment growth and output growth above the national average, but, productivity growth below the national average.
Source: Authors' own elaboration using data from Cambridge Econometrics.

https://doi.org/10.1080/2578711X.2021.1992168

across Britain have succeeded in achieving positive differential growth in *both* employment and productivity (the upper right quadrant in Figure 2.17).

2.6 CONCLUSIONS: THE SCALE AND GEOGRAPHIES OF THE "LEFT BEHIND" PROBLEM

Several key features emerge from this brief analysis of some of the basic dimensions of the UK's economic geography as mapped by the growth of employment, output, wages and productivity. First, on the basis of these four measures of economic performance, it is clear that the UK regions, cities, towns and rural communities have pulled apart over the past four to five decades, and especially since the beginning of the 1980s, as the economy has undergone an historic shift from one regime of growth and development to another.

Second, the identification of "left behind" places is not straightforward. Much depends on the choice of key indicators. Different indicators do not necessarily map closely one with another: the rank order correlation of the UK's 370 LADs on each the four main variables surveyed in this chapter reveals this weak correspondence (Table 2.3). The two measures that show the clearest correlation across localities are employment growth and output growth. Other correlations are much lower in comparison.

Third, on every indicator, it is possible to identify "left behind places" not just in the "North", but also in some parts of the "South", including certain London boroughs. Current UK government statements about "levelling up" the economic geography of the country have played especially to the problem of Northern towns and smaller cities, the constituencies that the Conservatives captured from Labour in the 2019 General Election (many of which also voted strongly for Brexit). It is clear, however, that any "levelling up" agenda that ignores those Southern localities that have also not shared fully in national prosperity over recent decades runs the political risk of losing what in many of these areas has traditionally been

Table 2.3 Spearman rank order correlations between different dimensions of local economic performance (cumulative percentage point differential growth), 1981–2018:

	Employment	GVA	Productivity	Real wages
Employment	1.000	0.703	−0.202	0.183
GVA		1.000	0.398	0.320
Productivity			1.000	0.161
Real wages				1.000

Note: The Spearman rank correlation coefficient measures the degree to which local authority districts (LADs) have the same rankings on any two variables of interest. GVA, gross value added.

https://doi.org/10.1080/2578711X.2021.1992168

Conservative electoral support. But it is, nevertheless, in the "North" that most economically lagging localities are to be found. And among these are the majority of the core cities, the UK's major second-tier urban centres that played a key role in Britain's industrial past, and which remain the economic hubs of much of the North of the country.

Fourth, the widening growth gaps between "left behind" places and those that have "pulled ahead" are not some mere "accident of history". They derive from the self-perpetuating forces set in motion by structural, technological, competitive, institutional and policy changes as these have evolved over recent decades, and the differential ability and scope of different places to adapt to those changes. Understanding those changes is a key prerequisite for constructing decisive policy strategies capable of securing any significant degree of "levelling up" of "left behind places".

NOTES

[1] Hall P (1962) *The Industries of London since 1861*. London: Hutchinson, at 9.

[2] Our focus in this book is on the economic dimensions of becoming "left behind", and we fully acknowledge "left behind places" may also suffer from, and be defined by, a range of social, environmental and cultural disadvantages, which will also need to be the focus of policy. But many such problems—such as poor-quality housing, poor health, low educational achievement, poor air quality, run-down social infrastructures and a lack of cultural facilities—are inextricably bound up with the economic opportunities and prosperity of an area, as both consequences and causes.

[3] Streeck W (2016) *How Will Capitalism End? Essays on a Failing System*. London: Verso.

[4] Rosés J and Wolf N (2021) Regional growth and inequality in the long run: Europe, 1900–2015. *Oxford Review of Economic Policy*, 37: 17–48.

[5] Kemeny T and Storper M (2020) *Superstar Cities and Left Behind Places: Disruptive Innovation, Labour Demand and Inter-Regional Inequality* (Working Paper No. 41). LSE International Inequalities Institute.

[6] Sandbu M (2020) *The Economics of Belonging: A Radical Plan to Win Back the Left Behind and Achieve Prosperity for All*, pp. 50–70. Princeton: Princeton University Press.

[7] Sandbu (2020), pp. 71–92, see Reference 6.

[8] Rodrik D (2018) *Straight Talk on Trade: Ideas for a Sane World Economy*. Princeton: Princeton University Press.

[9] The "South" is defined as London, the South East, East of England (East Anglia), the South West and the East Midlands regions. The North comprises all other regions. Much of our empirical analysis refers to Britain, that is, the UK minus Northern Ireland, as consistent and comparable data for Northern Ireland are unfortunately not always available; Martin RL (1988) The political economy of Britain's North–South divide. *Transactions of the Institute of British Geographers*, n.s., 13: 389–418; Martin RL (2006) The contemporary debate over the North–South divide: Images and realities of regional inequality in late twentieth century Britain. In Baker ARH and Billinge M (eds.), *Geographies of England:*

The North–South Divide, Imagined and Material, pp. 15–43. Cambridge: Cambridge University Press; Smith D (1989) *North and South: Britain's Economic, Social and Political Divide*. London: Penguin; Lewis J and Townsend A (1989) *The North–South Divide: Regional Change in Britain in the 1980s*. London: Paul Chapman.

[10] Geary F and Stark T (2015) Regional GDP in the UK, 1861–1911: New estimates. *Economic History Review*, 68: 123–144; Geary F and Stark T (2016) What happened to regional inequality in Britain in the twentieth century? *Economic History Review*, 69: 215–222.

[11] The cumulative differential growth is the running sum over successive years of the difference between the percentage growth rate of a region's employment (or output) in each year minus the corresponding growth rate for the national economy as a whole in that year.

[12] Blanchard OJ and Katz F (1992) Regional evolutions. *Brookings Papers on Economic Activity*, 1: 1–61.

[13] London had been one of the country's largest industrial centres. At the beginning of the 1970s, it employed more than 1 million workers in manufacturing. Over the period 1971–91, it shed some 685,000 of those jobs. During those decades, London also experienced a substantial decline in its population, so that its relative per capita GDP actually rose (see Table 2.1).

[14] Martin RL (2013) London's economy: From resurgence to recession to rebalancing. In M Tewdwr-Jones, N Phelps and R Freestone (eds.), *The Planning Imagination: Peter Hall and the Study of Urban and Regional Planning*, pp. 67–84. London: Routledge.

[15] Jackman R and Savouri S (1999) Has Britain solved the "regional problem"? In P Gregg and J Wadsworth (eds.), *The State of Working Britain*, pp. 29–46. Manchester: Manchester University Press.

[16] HM Government (1997) *Sharing the Nation's Prosperity*, p. 7. London: Cabinet Office.

[17] It might be questioned why we focus on LADs on the grounds that they do not represent "functional economic areas". Travel-to-work areas (TTWAs) would be more meaningful in this sense, since they are intended to represent "self-contained" labour catchment areas. However, not only does the "self-containment" threshold used by the ONS to delimit TTWAs vary significantly (from 75% of those both working and living in the same area to as low as 66%), but also the definition of the TTWAs that span the UK has changed significantly several times over the past 40 years or so (there were 308 in 1991, 243 in 2001, and 228 in 2011), much more so than have LADs. Also, importantly, LADs are the official units that raise local business taxes, and which administer financial grants from central government for the delivery of a range of social services and functions. Further, and importantly, LADs are the spatial units eligible to apply for the UK government's new Levelling Up Fund (see https://assets. publishing.service.gov.uk/government/uploads/system/uploads/attachment_data/file/966138/ Levelling_Up_prospectus.pdf). While LADs have undoubted limitations as units of study, the 370 LADs do give a more granular picture of the country's economic geography than do the 228 TTWAs or the 38 English Local Enterprise Partnerships.

[18] Moretti E (2012) *The New Geography of Jobs*. Boston: Mariner; Storper M, Kemeny TY and Osman T (2015) *The Rise and Fall of Urban Economies: Lessons from San Francisco and Los Angeles*. Stanford, CA: Stanford Business Books; Hendrickson C, Muro M and Galston WA (2018) *Countering the Geography of Discontent: Strategies for Left Behind Places*. Washington, DC: Brookings Institution.

[19] Pike A (2018) The limits of city centrism? We need to rethink how we approach urban and regional development. *British Politics and Policy*, LSE online. https://blogs.lse.ac.uk/politicsandpolicy/ the-limits-of-city-centrism/

[20] Pike (2018), see Reference 19.

[21] Although, of course, high housing costs in the capital reduce this advantage. Very recently, however, cities such as Oxford, Cambridge and Winchester have had more unfavourable "affordability" indices than parts of London.

[22] Centre for Progressive Policy (2020) *Beyond Hard Hats: What It Will Take to Level Up The UK.* https://www.progressive-policy.net/publications/beyond-hard-hats/.

[23] Martin RL, Sunley PJ, Gardiner B, Evenhuis E and Tyler P (2018) The city dimension of the productivity growth puzzle: The relative roles of structural changes and within-sector slowdown. *Journal of Economic Geography*, 18: 539–570.

[24] Beatty C and Fothergill S (2019) *Local Productivity: The Real Differences across UK Cities and Regions.* Sheffield: Centre for Regional Economic and Social Research, Sheffield Hallam University.

[25] Cuadrado-Roura JR, Mancha-Navarro T and Garrido-Yserte R (2000) Regional productivity patterns in Europe: An alternative approach. *Annals of Regional Science*, 34: 365–384.

3. WHY PLACES HAVE FALLEN BEHIND: THE GEOGRAPHICALLY UNEVEN EFFECTS OF ECONOMIC TRANSFORMATION

Keywords: Economic transformation, deindustrialization, post-industrial economy, knowledge-intensive services, public sector, local skills

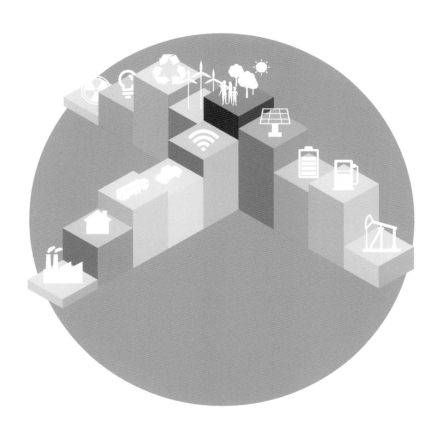

The significance of deindustrialization can therefore be evaluated only in terms of how rapidly and how successfully workers dislocated from so-called sunset industries are reemployed in growing, sunrise industries.[1]

3.1 EVOLVING GEOGRAPHIES OF ECONOMIC TRANSFORMATION

As Chapter 2 explained, during the past four decades or so, advanced countries have experienced a switch from spatial convergence and the gradual decline of spatial inequalities to an era of divergence and growing regional and local inequalities. The intensification of divergence has been such that it is no exaggeration to say that it has become a force tearing at the cohesion and collective belonging of Western liberal societies.[2] There have been a growing number of attempts to understand the economic forces behind this increase in spatial inequalities. There is some agreement that the rapid progress of technological change together with globalization and the growth of consumer and business services have been crucial. Together, such forces have produced an era of economic turmoil and "creative destruction" as some manufacturing industries have declined while other service sectors have grown rapidly. This round of "creative destruction" has had profoundly uneven geographical dimensions, and some places have lost their economic rationale, while others have found new roles and sources of value creation.

This chapter examines how the spatial distribution of employment growth has changed in this unstable period of transition, and which types of area have struggled to capture significant employment growth. While the recent literature has emphasized the rise of new agglomerations of knowledge-intensive growth, there is also the need to understand the selective and uneven growth of more dispersed service and other activities, which have shown a preference for smaller settlements. Further, it emerges that reinforcing dynamics in population and labour market processes have intensified the problems of different types of "left behind" area. Although much current research and policy discussion in the UK highlight the problems of towns, it is also necessary to consider the combined regional and urban dimensions to employment change. We find that the most severe cumulative employment failures are in Northern urban areas, and particularly in the large and core cities, as well as former industrial towns. The chapter concludes by examining how these processes have been closely related to cumulative dynamics in population change and skill patterns, which have entrenched the disadvantages of types of falling behind place.

https://doi.org/10.1080/2578711X.2021.1992169

3.2 POST-INDUSTRIAL SPACES OF GROWTH AND DECLINE

The wider processes of change associated with the "Great Divergence" discussed in Chapter 2 have been playing out in particular ways in the UK. It has been argued that London has followed a highly globalized economic path that is increasingly decoupled and disconnected from the rest of the UK economy.[3] Despite their different emphases, most of these studies suggest that this new era of geographical divergence is driven by new dynamics of geographical concentration and agglomeration. Sandbu, for example, assigns particular importance to the way that an agglomerated form of economic growth has undermined the spread of prosperity and the "economics of belonging":

> the economic transformation of the past forty years has shifted the engine of value creation from a territorially spread out system of labour-intensive industrial production to more concentrated activity of knowledge-based and high-tech services. Regional convergence has long since stalled or gone in the reverse.[4]

In this view, the agglomeration of knowledge-intensive service and digital industries has meant that fewer places have been able to access the rewards of this new engine of prosperity.

However, while there is no doubt that some forms of agglomeration have been important, several other key geographical trends have significantly changed the form of the post-industrial economic landscape. In fact, the contemporary post-industrial economy has involved two forms of modes of growth. The first, which, as noted in Chapter 2, is widely recognized in the literature, is a highly concentrated type of high-knowledge growth, and there is a wealth of literature that has begun to explain why these agglomerations arise in some places and not others.[5] The second type of growth that has received much less attention is a more distributed and spatially dispersed type of growth, which is evident in both many service sectors and advanced manufacturing. Of course, the so-called "urban–rural shift" was first identified in the 1980s,[6] and somewhat later the regionalized mode of growth of services across South East England was also highlighted.[7] However, in recent decades it has tended to be assumed that an era of "urban triumph" means that this shift is no longer relevant. Yet, this interpretation is far too simplistic. While the second form of service sector growth is more dispersed, it is integral to the creative destruction of places seen over past decades, and far from being no longer relevant it continues to shape the economic fortunes of cities, towns and regions. In the case of Britain, we will see that even though it is more spatially dispersed than the agglomerative form of growth, it is nevertheless locationally selective, shaped by consumer spending, and has led to a significant and forceful shift of growth into some smaller cities, towns and rural areas.

3.3 THE CHANGING LOCATION OF EMPLOYMENT

To understand these two forms of spatial change, we start by examining key structural changes in the geography of employment. In Britain's case, it is undoubtedly true that the disappearance of manufacturing jobs through technological change and globalization has undermined the productivity, employment and export bases of many former manufacturing heartlands.[8] The fall in manufacturing employment has been felt most strongly in traditionally industrial regions such as the North East, North West and West Midlands, but also in London; in these areas total production employment has fallen by more than half.[9] There is also a discernible pattern to deindustrialization across settlement types (Figure 3.1). Production employment has fallen most in the major cities and larger towns. There has been a slight increase in production employment since the 2008–10 great recession, but this seems to have been concentrated mainly in London and rural areas. In comparison, the upturn in production employment in the major core cities and other cities has been much less.

In fact, contrary to much current rhetoric about city resurgence and revival through the strengthening of high-technology clusters of advanced manufacturing firms, manufacturing employment has continued to undergo an urban–rural shift and many parts of knowledge-intensive manufacturing have grown in semi-urban areas and small towns.[10] The same

Figure 3.1 Decline in production employment across British cities and towns, 1981–2018 (indexed 1981 = 100)

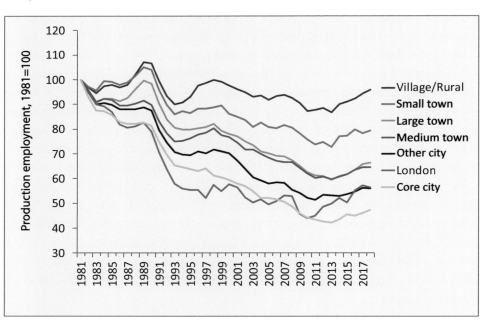

Source: Authors' own elaboration using data from Cambridge Econometrics.

spatial dynamic of long-term geographical dispersal has been reported in other countries.[11] Just as the boundaries between manufacturing and service industries have become increasingly blurred with "servitization" and the fragmentation of value chains into functions, stages and tasks, so the locational preferences of knowledge-intensive manufacturing and service industries have become less distinct. Foreign direct investors in manufacturing have preferred to locate in non-traditionally industrial cities and towns and have invested to an increasing degree in Southern regions with better residential environments, more educated workforces and better transport connectivity.[12] Such geographical differentiation in the experiences of places across the UK has important implications for institutional and policy responses (see Chapter 5).

3.4 THE RISE OF KNOWLEDGE-INTENSIVE BUSINESS SERVICES (KIBS)

The growth of KIBS has been a powerful force for divergence that again combines both regional and local dynamics, operating in conjunction. At a local scale, there is evidence of a shift from cities to towns and rural areas, especially in Southern regions outside of London (Figure 3.2).

Figure 3.2 Growth in knowledge-intensive business services (KIBS) employment across British cities and towns, 1981–2018 (indexed 1981 = 100)

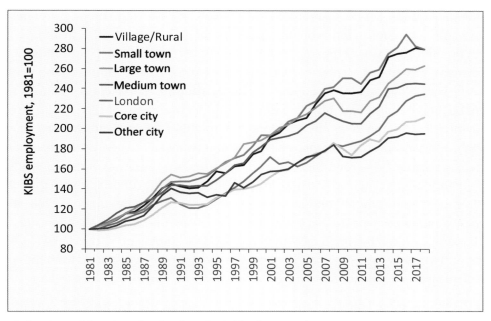

Source: Authors' own elaboration using data from Cambridge Econometrics.

Table 3.1 Shares of total employment change in each sector by type of local authority district (LAD), 1981–2018

	KIBS (% of total growth)	Other private services (% of total growth)	Public services (% of total growth)	Production (% of total decline)
London	26.60%	9.55%	11.41%	15.05%
Large town	21.38%	25.09%	22.48%	23.90%
Village/rural	14.94%	28.07%	19.41%	1.95%
Medium town	12.16%	16.16%	12.17%	17.68%
Core city	12.00%	5.63%	13.55%	20.00%
Other city	7.61%	6.74%	13.82%	16.73%
Small town	5.31%	8.75%	7.17%	4.68%
Total	100.0%	100.0%	100.0%	100.0%

Note: KIBS, knowledge-intensive business services.*Source*: Authors' own elaboration using data from Cambridge Econometrics.

This fast growth has meant that cities apart from London have captured a remarkably low share of KIBS employment growth over the period (Table 3.1).

London, of course, already had a marked specialization in these services at the start of the period. However, as shown in Chapter 2, it has grown output (gross value added—GVA) in these activities much faster than employment, which helps to explain its high productivity. London has benefitted from the huge growth of output and wealth in financial and other professional business services, and these have driven up its average productivity per head and its wages. However, in terms of KIBS employment over the 1981–2018 period, London's growth up until 2008 was comparable with other large cities in Britain. Since then, its KIBS employment growth has accelerated away from the other cities, demonstrating the unexpected resilience of parts of the London economy after the global crash. But, as it will be shown, London has also had much weaker growth in other types of service and transport employment before the 2008 crash (Figure 3.4). Together, these trends are key causes of London's profound problem of internal spatial inequalities between boroughs, shown in Chapter 2. In terms of job growth, it is misleading to describe the city as undergoing a "superstar trajectory" that is divorced and uncoupled from other large conurbations in the country. In KIBS employment growth, London has been similar to other cities up until 2008, and it is only in the recovery since 2010 that it has performed markedly better than other cities. Since 1981, London has seen the rapid growth of professional employment, but many low-skilled groups, and a rapidly growing immigrant population, have been excluded from the growth of good quality, well-paid jobs.[13]

Figure 3.3 throws more light onto the growth of KIBS across the country as it plots the total growth of KIBS employment against the total growth of other employment (both minus the

 https://doi.org/10.1080/2578711X.2021.1992169

Figure 3.3 Differential growth of employment in knowledge-intensive business services (KIBS) and other (non-production) industries by local authority districts (LADs), 1981–2018

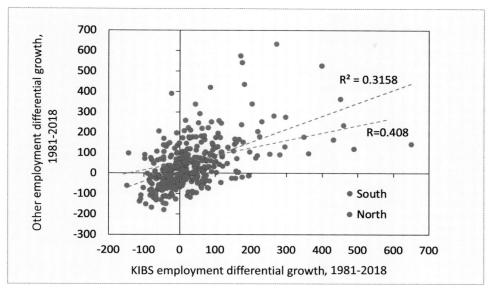

Source: Authors' own elaboration using data from Cambridge Econometrics.

total national rate) for both Southern and Northern local authority districts (LADs).[14] Several features are worth noting. First, some LADs, mostly in the South, but also a subset of Northern LADs, have raced ahead of the pack in terms of KIBS jobs growth. Second, the relationships between KIBS growth and other service growth are only modest, so that some LADs have seen strong growth in other labour-intensive services without strong KIBS growth, and vice versa. This relationship is noticeably weaker in Northern LADs, so it appears that KIBS growth has not been sufficient in many Northern LADs to lead a drive to wider and more general growth across a broad range of service industries. While many Northern LADs have lost their manufacturing engines of jobs growth, these have not been replaced by business service engines that are forceful enough to replace the jobs benefits of manufacturing.

The pattern of growth of these lower value and labour-intensive services, which have accounted for by far the largest part of employment growth, differs from that of KIBS because it appears to follow a more dispersed pattern. As a consequence, over the whole period 1981–2018, the share of other service growth in London and the core cities is strikingly low (Table 3.1). The rate of growth has been stronger in rural areas and smaller towns and, somewhat surprisingly, weaker in large cities and urban areas (Figure 3.4). While many rural and semi-rural areas, and towns, have seen the growth of lower skill service activities, core cities and London have tended to see much lower rates of employment growth, and this has had a significant impact on their overall job creation. Other cities have fared little

Figure 3.4 Other (non-knowledge-intensive business services—KIBS) private service employment growth across British cities and towns, 1981–2018 (indexed 1981 = 100)

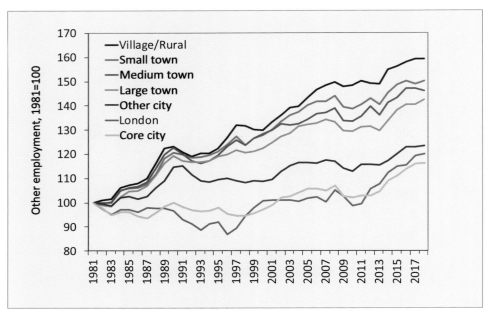

Source: Authors' own elaboration using data from Cambridge Econometrics.

better. Employment growth in other private services has been stronger in villages and small settlements and in large towns, while their growth in large regional cities has been small.

3.5 A PUBLIC SECTOR COUNTER-WEIGHT?

Traditionally, the public sector has served as a "buffer" to local economic instability and a bulwark against rapid decline, being relatively immune to cyclical and other disruptions to the labour market. An interesting question, then, is whether and to what degree the expansion of public sector employment has offset and compensated for the spatially uneven patterns of private sector transformation? Figure 3.5 shows how the growth of public sector employment has been much slower since the 2008 crash, with the notable exception of London. While public sector employment growth stalled in many areas after the global recession, in large part because of the austerity measures and expenditure reductions imposed on the public sector by the Government, its growth in London actually accelerated. This was a striking reversal of the pattern seen during the 1990s, when public sector employment was falling rapidly in London but growing steadily elsewhere. What is also evident is that public service employment growth has followed the relative shift of economic activity and movement of

Figure 3.5 Public services employment growth across British cities and towns, 1981–2018 (indexed 1981 = 100)

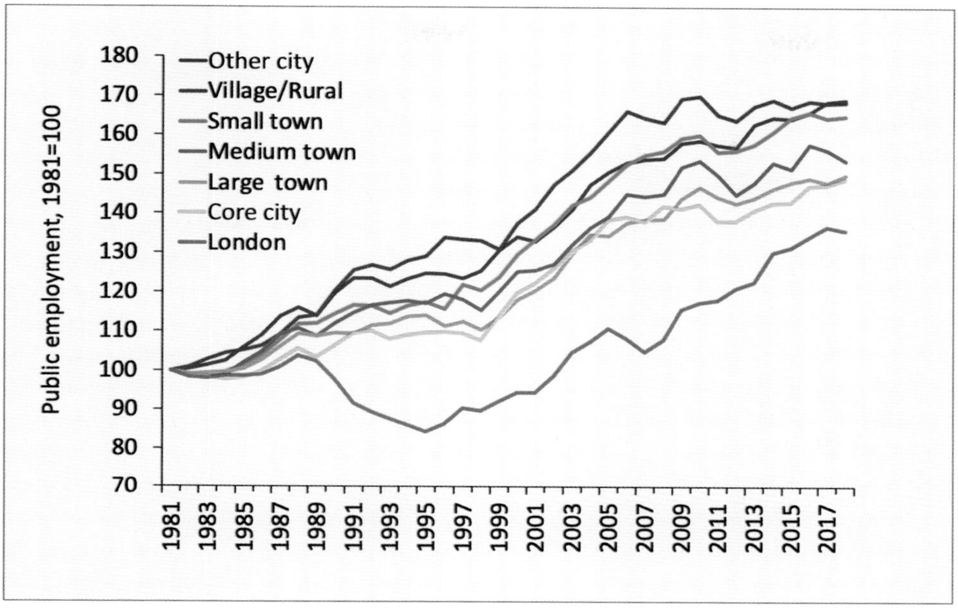

Source: Authors' own elaboration using data from Cambridge Econometrics.

population to small towns and rural areas, and other cities, and has not compensated for the relative weakness of private service sector job growth in the core cities.

3.6 A COMBINED URBAN AND REGIONAL PROBLEM

In the case of Britain, then, the transformation towards a post-industrial economic landscape has intensified geographical inequalities through the worsening of both regional and urban problems. Both knowledge- and labour-intensive service growth have discriminated between places and regions, and reworked the pattern of economic advantage through concentration in some places but dispersal to other types of place. The combined outcomes of these intersecting processes are captured by Figure 3.6, which shows the cumulative differential employment growth in Northern LADs by settlement type. For this part of Britain, a rural–urban hierarchy is evident with only village or smaller settlements having seen employment growth above the national average, and small towns have, until recently, been matching this national average. The long-run employment performance of core and other cities, and medium towns, has been especially poor in Northern regions. While there was a relative improvement in employment growth in Northern core cities from the late 1990s, this was brought to a halt by the global financial crisis and recession from 2008. Although their differential growth rate has improved more recently,

Figure 3.6 Cumulative differential total employment growth gaps in Northern local authority districts (LADs) by settlement type, 1981–2018

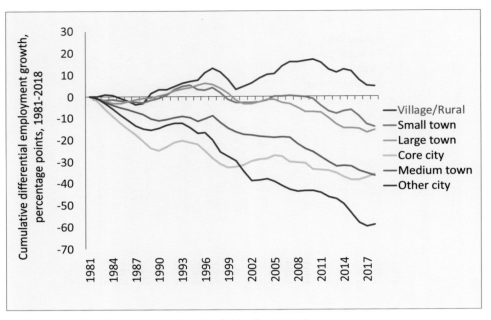

Source: Authors' own elaboration using data from Cambridge Econometrics.

nevertheless by 2018 employment in Northern cities was between 30 and 50 percentage points below what it would have been if they followed the national rate of jobs growth.

In contrast, as Figure 3.7 shows, most types of LAD in Southern regions have seen employment growth above the national average and, once again, smaller settlements have tended to see faster relative jobs growth. Cumulative employment growth in towns in the South is now between 50% and 80% above national growth. Employment in villages/rural areas in the South has grown around 60 percentage points above the national average, which is in stark contrast with other cities in the North that have seen cumulative employment growth of 60 percentage points below the national rate. While the employment performance of some Northern towns has clearly been relatively poor, this should not overshadow the fact that Northern cities have been doubly disadvantaged by both regional and urban–rural processes and, in aggregate, their jobs performance has unambiguously been the worst record of all places.

Some insight into the causes behind this substantial divergence in employment performance across LADs and types of settlement can be gained using dynamic shift–share analysis. This decomposes employment growth into a "national effect", which shows what would have happened if all of a locality's sectors had grown at the national rate; an "industry structure effect", which shows whether places have tended to specialize in nationally fast- or slow-growing industries; and a local "competitiveness effect", which measures how a locality's industries

Figure 3.7 **Cumulative differential total employment growth gaps in Southern local authority districts (LADs) by settlement type, 1981–2018**

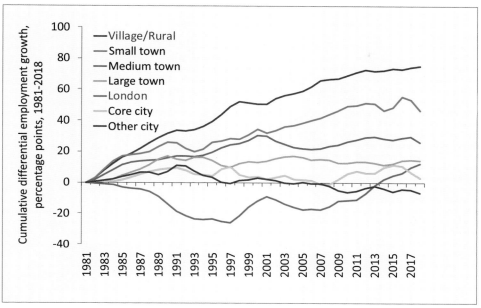

Source: Authors' own elaboration using data from Cambridge Econometrics.

have grown faster or slower than their national counterparts.[15] Our recent research has indicated that as manufacturing has declined, so the industry specializations of different areas have become more similar over time, so that the place-based "competitiveness" residual effect has become more significant.[16] Figure 3.8 shows that "competitiveness" effects have actually been negative in both London and the core cities, indicating that industries in large and dense urban areas have performed less well than the same industries in other types of area. It appears that only London has experienced a significant structural benefit from specialization in faster growing industries, while the positive structural effect in core cities has been much smaller. Competitiveness effects are negative in other cities, but positive in small towns and rural areas. In terms of employment growth, agglomeration benefits in cities appear not to have been so dominant or influential as commonly assumed and asserted, and that they have been tempered by various and related diseconomies. As we have discussed elsewhere, the causes of these residual (positive and negative) competitiveness effects are likely to be varied.

Many studies highlight the importance of the level of education of the labour force and the presence of high-skilled occupations and groups.[17] Other causes may also include such factors as the strength of local innovation, the connectivity of the area and character of infrastructure, the quality of the residential environment, the cost and flexibility of housing, and the availability of appropriate business properties. But there are clearly features of non-urban and smaller settlements that have tended to generate and attract the faster growing types of firms within

Figure 3.8 Shift–share decomposition of employment change by local authority district (LAD) type, 1981–2018

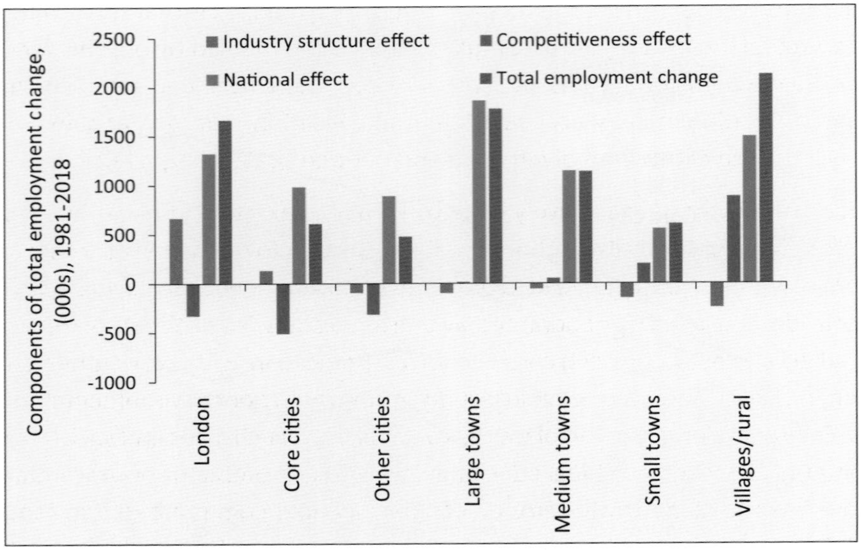

Source: Authors' own elaboration using data from Cambridge Econometrics.

industries, especially in Southern regions. Those places with better quality residential environments, better connectivity and increasing populations appear to have markedly stronger employment dynamism.

While locational needs vary with business models, these findings suggest that rural and small town locations are offering significant advantages to a wide range of firms. However, the evaluation of these place-specific competitive effects is complicated by the fact that new patterns of unbundled specialization within value networks may mean that places may well be specializing by task and function within each industry. If this is the case, then these new forms of specialization may be increasing the importance of these place-specific "competitiveness effects" and the spatial distribution of types of activity, and this will drive more uneven geographical growth over time.[18]

3.7 CUMULATIVE PROCESSES AND VICIOUS CIRCLES

These outcomes indicate that the transformation of Britain's economy since the 1980s has not only exposed the differential vulnerabilities of cities and regions to processes of manufacturing decline and service growth, but also that regions and local economies have proved to have marked variations in their capacities to respond and adapt to these ongoing pressures and shifts. The problems of adaptation and response have evidently been most severe in

https://doi.org/10.1080/2578711X.2021.1992169

Northern cities and urban areas, and are strongly manifested in their employment dynamics, so that the country now faces a severe problem of uneven geographical development and spatial disparities. The real challenge for any "levelling up" policy is that these differences in economic adaptability are long term, cumulative and often marked by positive feedbacks so that initial differences become wider over time. Indeed, there has been a growing awareness of these processes of cumulative causation and a realization that relying solely on market processes will tend to exacerbate divergence and deepen spatial inequalities.

In recent years, there has been relatively little work on how exactly these reinforcing processes work in "left behind places", although it is well known that low employment rates and poor employment conditions frequently lead to problems of poverty, inequality, poor health and other types of social deprivation. The geographically uneven distributional effects of the workings of housing markets and public housing construction and allocation act to concentrate problems of unemployment, low skill and economic insecurity in areas with poor environmental and housing conditions. Emergent deprivation in places has an effect on life chances and social mobility that goes beyond the effects of individual education levels.[19] Such problems of concentrated disadvantage have been worsened by the erosion of public services, community life and social capital in many of these most deprived areas. The decline in many towns of their high streets and the disappearance of local leisure and community facilities has been found to have a strong negative effect on local perceptions of well-being and pride of place.[20] Partly for these reasons, there have been a growing number of calls for regeneration policies that focus more on restoring the "foundational economy" of basic services and social care to "left behind" areas (see Chapter 7).

There is little doubt that population change and movement play a key role in these processes of cumulative disadvantage. In poorer areas, those who want to move on also tend to be those who move out.[21] While rates of out-migration from "left behind" areas in Britain are low and restricted by "steep cliffs" in house price differentials in more prosperous places, those who do move out tend to be younger and more educated. Even those who move to other economically depressed local areas tend to benefit from greater wage progression.[22] Figure 3.9 shows the population trends in the 74 most poorly performing LADs in terms of employment and output (identified in Table 2.2 in Chapter 2), classified by their settlement type. Important differences between the population trajectories that exist in cities as against other types of falling behind places. While the struggling urban areas have seen population growth since the turn of the century (and earlier in London's case), other "left behind" places such as large and medium towns have seen only marginal growth. The population totals of these areas have been broadly stagnant. In these areas and in the core cities, growth since the turn of the century has only reversed the loss of population seen before 2000.

Table 3.2 examines the underlying components of population change in the 74 lowest employment growth LADs in the period of growth between 2001 and 2019. The much higher rates of population growth in "left behind" LADs in cities are evident. It also shows that these

Figure 3.9 Indexed population growth in the bottom 74 local authority districts (LADs) (by employment and output) by settlement type, 1981–2018

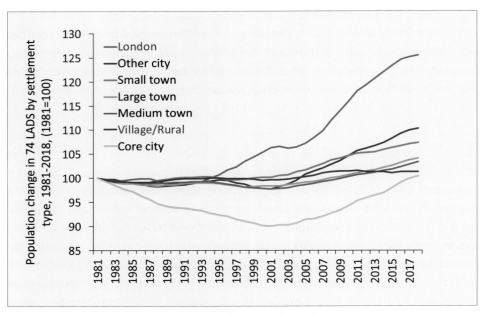

Note: For the list of the 74 worse-performing LADs see Table 2.2 in Chapter 2.
Source: Authors' own elaboration using data from the Office for National Statistics (ONS).

areas suffer from very high negative net internal migration, but this is offset by high international net migration and high natural growth. Of course, this combination of population growth and low employment growth creates severe wage and productivity problems. In the other types of "left behind" towns, however, population changes are much more subdued.

Table 3.2 Components of population change in the bottom 74 local authority districts (LADs) (by employment and output) by settlement type, 2001–18:

	% Total change	Natural net (%)	Net internal migration (%)	Net international migration (%)	Other change (%)[a]
London	18.40%	19.22%	−25.67%	21.56%	3.29%
Other city	12.85%	8.84%	−8.9%	11.35%	1.55%
Core city	12.80%	7.0%	−7.78%	12.07%	1.56%
Small town	7.71%	0.37%	4.58%	1.01%	1.75%
Large town	6.14%	1.61%	1.11%	3.07%	0.34%
Medium town	5.58%	0.4%	2.85%	1.49%	0.84%
Village/rural	1.89%	−3.08%	5.09%	−0.63%	0.5%

Note: For the 74 LADs classified by settlement type, see Table 2.2 in Chapter 2.[a]Other change includes movements in special groups such as prisoners and members of the armed forces and other unattributed changes.Source: Data are from the Office for National Statistics (ONS).

Both their net natural growth and net internal migration are low, and these types of areas have not attracted large net inward flows from international migration, so that they face more severe problems of population shrinkage. In population terms, there are two quite distinct types of "left behind" area which face quite different problems in terms of attracting population and providing services that respond to population growth or stagnation. "Left behind" areas outside of the cities have failed to benefit from strong net internal and international migration, and the underlying reasons for this situation deserve much more detailed investigation. Once again, it is essential to recognize that the "left behind" label covers a variety of places with specific and distinctive challenges, so that generalizations about the population dynamics of "left behind" places are inevitably misrepresentations if they ignore this heterogeneity.

These varied population dynamics have also been closely linked to vicious cycles in the development of human capital and spatial sorting of skill groups. Deprived areas have become trapped in low-skill positions in which the demand for low skills and lower wage work becomes matched over time by a local labour supply of these skills.[23] Such areas experience a net inflow of low-skilled groups and a net outflow of the higher skilled.[24] If these circular dynamics are unbroken, initiatives and policies to raise the skills of local residents may simply lead to those residents moving to more skilled local labour markets elsewhere. One of the key lasting effects of deindustrialization has been that processes of labour market "hollowing out" and the decline of middle-skilled occupations have been found to be much stronger in Northern regions and cities.[25] While Northern urban areas have undoubtedly benefitted from the national trends towards more skilled and professional occupations, their rate of growth of these occupations has been lower than nationally. Indeed, their labour markets have become strongly bifurcated as low-skilled occupations in sectors such as retail, hospitality and care have grown most rapidly, while middle-skilled machine operative, technically oriented and medium-skilled service occupations have declined. The decline of manufacturing employment has eroded many middle-skilled occupations and this has had important effects on social mobility. Furthermore, as we have seen, there appears to be large parts of the semi-skilled service economy that is barely growing in Northern cities.

These processes have thus produced a widening divergence in skills between local economies in Northern and Southern Britain. Figure 3.10 compares the share of employment in LADs in high-skilled occupational groups in 1991 with the share in the high-skilled groups in 2011. Not only has the relationship been highly stable over time, but also most LADs in Northern regions show lower high-skill shares, and only a few exceptions have significantly increased their high-skill shares. The distribution for Southern LADs is very stretched, and a small minority of Southern areas have remined very low skilled. At the other end of the distribution, however, some Southern localities have reinforced their initial advantage. This confirms the idea that post-industrial growth involves a more selective and differentiated geographical pattern in which some "hotspot" agglomerations and clusters pull away from

Figure 3.10 Share of employment in high-skill occupations in local authority districts (LADs), 1991 and 2011

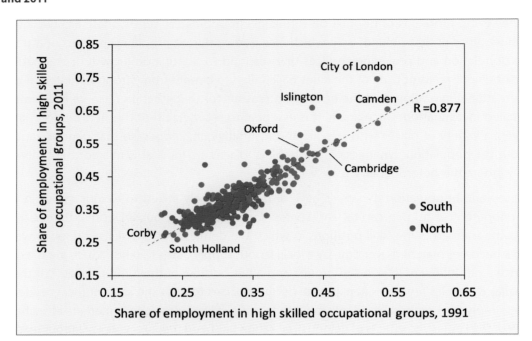

Source: Authors' own elaboration using data from Cambridge Econometrics. High skill occupations are in Skill Level 4 based on SOC10 Occupational Groups.

many others. One or two Northern LADs could be said to potential candidates to move into this high-performing group, but most show a much lower high-skill occupational share. Indeed, a set of high-skill areas in the North had lost share by 2011, presumably as their manufacturing production has declined.

Figure 3.11 shows the distribution of shares in low-skilled occupational groups in 1991 and 2011, and it provides almost a mirror image of Figure 3.10. While a few Southern LADs have very high low-skill shares, the majority have a relatively low prevalence of low-skilled occupations, and again there is a stretched pattern in which many Southern areas are well above, and moving further away from, the national average. In contrast, many Northern LADs have low-skill shares above 40%, and seem stuck in that position.

3.8 CONCLUSIONS: UNDERSTANDING HOW PLACES HAVE BECOME "LEFT BEHIND"

The complex pattern of "left behind places" across Britain reflects similarly complex patterns in the geographical distribution of "post-industrial" employment growth. Two fundamental

 https://doi.org/10.1080/2578711X.2021.1992169

Figure 3.11 Share of employment in low-skill occupations by local authority districts (LADs), 1991 and 2011

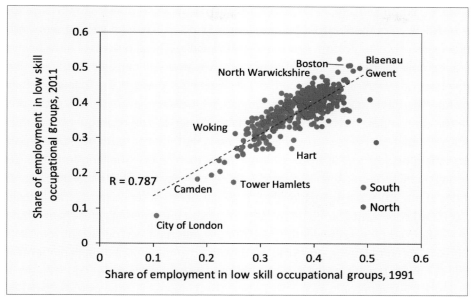

Source: Authors' own elaboration using data from Cambridge Econometrics. Low skill groups are in Skill Level 1 based on SOC10 Occupational groups.

modes of growth in the post-industrial economy are discernible. The first is knowledge-intensive and agglomerated, while the second is dispersed and spreading a wide profile of service employment, but in a highly spatially uneven and discriminatory fashion—at both regional and local scales. Recent analyses of the spaces of economic growth in this era of divergence have been dominated by the first mode, and have given insufficient thought to selective dispersal and to the reasons why, with greater locational choice, it is shifting economic growth away from formerly industrial Northern regions, and especially from cities and towns in these regions. In the UK case, and in contrast to the rhetoric on cities, most big cities have struggled to generate enough employment, and even some parts of London have not been immune from this problem. Agglomeration has been only one part of place effects, and it is much less important in this second type of growth. The economic quality and reputations of places and their living environments are increasingly essential to their economic fortunes as much post-industrial growth has become potentially more footloose and with greater locational choice, but it has proved to be more discerning of location and place effects. In the UK, the combination of these patterns means that the core cities and industrial towns in Northern regions have shown very weak employment growth over four decades. The relative weakness of innovative high-knowledge agglomerations in such areas is evident and, moreover, their development has not been sufficiently strong to spark wider employment growth.

"Left behind places" exist across the UK, including some London boroughs, and former ports and coastal areas in the South, but nevertheless the pattern of disadvantage in the UK in dominated by a combined urban *and* regional problem. Northern towns and cities, many in large conurbations in the North West, the North East and in Central Scotland, have shown long-term and cumulative processes of strikingly poor economic performance. These processes have been closely related to cumulative dynamics in population change and skill patterns, and have produced key differences between different types of "falling behind" place. In the following chapter we examine how this has impacted on the economic and social resilience of many urban areas and whether this unevenness has been exposed and worsened by the consequences of the Covid-19 pandemic. What is now particularly concerning is that the consequences of the pandemic and subsequent recovery are likely to reinforce rather than reverse the long-term spatial trends documented in this Chapter and in Chapter 2. There well may be a shift of balance between the two modes of growth and a greater impetus to the dispersal of service and other activities, but this will certainly continue to be highly spatially selective. Fundamentally, this chapter has shown that the trends in employment over the past four decades has been persistent, reinforcing and hard to break. The cumulative nature of locally diverging employment growth paths means that it is overly optimistic to believe that they will be countered by market corrections alone. Instead, it will require a substantial policy effort to address the complexity and entrenched nature of the UK's problem with "left behind places" and the national government's "levelling up" agenda.

NOTES

[1] Bluestone B (1984) Is deindustrialization a myth? Capital mobility versus absorptive capacity in the U.S. economy. *Annals of the American Academy of Political and Social Sciences*, 475: 39–51.

[2] Collier P (2018) *The Future of Capitalism: Facing the New Anxieties*. London: Allen Lane; Rodríguez-Pose A (2018) The revenge of the places that don't matter (and what to do about it). *Cambridge Journal of Regions, Economy and Society*, 11: 189–209; Sandbu M (2020) *The Economics of Belonging: A Radical Plan to Win Back the Left Behind and Achieve Prosperity for All*. Princeton: Princeton University Press.

[3] Deutsche Bank (2013) *London and the UK Economy: In for a Penny, In for a Pound?* London: Deutsche Bank Markets Research; McCann P (2016) *The UK Regional–National Economic Problem*. London: Routledge; UK2070 Commission (2019) *Fairer and Stronger: Rebalancing the UK Economy*. London: UK2070.

[4] Sandbu (2020), p. 189, see Reference 2.

[5] Moretti E (2012) *The New Geography of Jobs*. Boston: Mariner; Florida R, Mellander C and King K (2017) *Winner Take All Cities* (Martin Prosperity Research Working Paper No. 2017-MP1WP-002); McKinsey Global Institute (2018) *Superstars: The Dynamics of Firms, Sectors and Cities Leading the Global Economy*. www.mckinsey.com/mgi; Crescenzi R, Iammarino S, Ioramashvili C, Rodríguez-Pose A and Storper M (2020) *The Geography of Innovation and Development: Global Spread and Local Hotspots* (Papers in Economic Geography and Spatial Economics). London: LSE.

6 Fothergill S and Gudgin G (1982) *Unequal Growth: Urban and Regional Employment Change in the UK*. London: Heinemann Educational; Keeble D and Tyler P (1995) Enterprising behaviour and the urban–rural shift. *Urban Studies*, 32: 975–997.

7 Allen J (1992) Services and the UK space economy: Regionalization and economic dislocation. *Transactions of the Institute of British Geographers*, 17: 292–305; Coe N and Townsend A (2004) Debunking the myth of localized agglomerations: The development of a regionalized service economy in South-East England. *Transactions of the Institute of British Geographers*, 23: 1–20.

8 Rowthorn B (2010) Combined and uneven development: Reflections on the North–South divide. *Spatial Economic Analysis*, 5: 363–388.

9 Production employment is defined as manufacturing plus the construction, mining, utilities and energy sectors.

10 Sunley P, Evenhuis E, Harris J, Harris R, Martin RL and Pike A (2021) Renewing industrial regions? Advanced manufacturing and industrial policy in Britain. *Regional Studies*. https://doi.org/10.1080/00343404.2021.1983163.

11 Crafts N and Klein A (2021) Spatial concentration of manufacturing industries in the United States: Re-examination of long-run trends. *European Review of Economic History*, 25: 223–246; Dauth W, Fuchs M and Otto A (2016) Long-run processes of geographical concentration and dispersal: Evidence from Germany. *Papers in Regional Science*, 97: 569–593.

12 Wren C and Jones J (2012) FDI location across British regions and agglomerative forces: A Markov analysis. *Spatial Economic Analysis* 7: 265–286; Sunley et al. (2021), see Reference 10.

13 Martin RL (2013) London's economy: From resurgence to recession to rebalancing. In M Tewdwr-Jones, N Phelps and R Freestone (eds.), *The Planning Imagination: Peter Hall and the Study of Urban and Regional Planning*, ch. 6. London: Routledge.

14 The other category includes all non-KIBS and non-production sectors and is dominated by retail and wholesale services and transport.

15 Rather than simply keeping a locality's industrial structure at the start year (here, 1981) constant throughout the period of analysis (1981–2018), as in ordinary shift–share analysis, in the dynamic version the analysis is conducted one year at a time, allowing the structure to vary accordingly, and the annual components of change are cumulated over successive years.

16 Martin RL, Sunley P, and Gardiner B (2016). How regions react to recession: Resistance, recoverability and resilience. *Regional Studies*, 50: 561–585; Martin RL, Sunley P, Gardiner B, Evenhuis E, and Tyler P (2018) The city dimension of the productivity growth puzzle: The relative role of structural change and within-sector slowdown. *Journal of Economic Geography*, 18: 539–570.

17 Huggins R and Thompson P (eds.) (2017) *Handbook of Regions and Competitiveness*. Cheltenham: Edward Elgar.

18 Baldwin R (2016) *The Great Convergence: Information Technology and the New Globalization*. Cambridge, MA: Harvard University Press; Martin et al. (2018), see Reference 16; Gervais A, Markusen J and Venables A (2021) *Urban Specialisation from Sectoral to Functional* (Working Paper No. 28352). Cambridge, MA: National Bureau of Economic Research (NBER). http://www.nber.org/papers/w28352/.

19 Social Mobility Commission (SMC) (2019) *Social Mobility in Great Britain—State of the Nation 2018 to 2019*. London: HMSO; Social Mobility Commission (SMC) (2020) *Moving Out to Move On: Understanding the Link between Migration, Disadvantage and Social Mobility*. London: IES.

20 Kenny M and Kelsey T (2021) *Levelling Up Britain's Towns*. UK in a Changing Europe. ukandeu.ac.uk/.

21 SMC (2019, 2020), see Reference 19.

22 SMC (2019, 2020), see Reference 19.

23 Sissons P (2021) The local low skills equilibrium: Moving from concept to policy utility. *Urban Studies*, 58: 1543–1560.

24 Fenton A, Tyler P, Markkanen S, Clarke A and Whitehead C (2010) *Why Do Neighbourhoods Stay Poor? Deprivation, Place and People in Birmingham*. London: Barrow Cadbury Trust.

25 Sunley P, Martin R, Gardiner B and Pike A (2020) In search of the skilled city: Skills and the occupational evolution of British cities. *Urban Studies*, 57: 109–133.

https://doi.org/10.1080/2578711X.2021.1992169

4. ECONOMIC SHOCKS AND THE DIFFERENTIAL RESILIENCE OF PLACES

Keywords: economic shocks, recessions, resilience, recoverability, Brexit, Covid pandemic

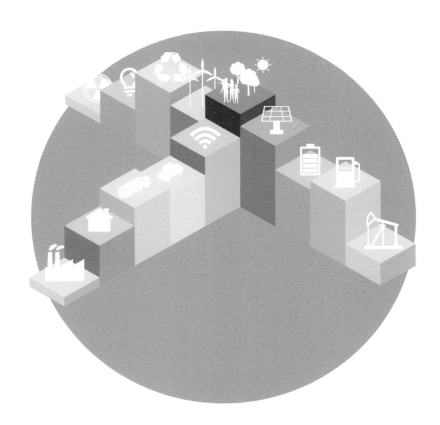

4.1 LOCAL ECONOMIC DEVELOPMENT AS A SHOCK-PRONE PROCESS

As Chapter 3 shows, two modes of uneven post-industrial growth have combined to produce a dramatic widening in inequalities in economic performance and well-being across the country. This change has left many Northern towns and cities, plus parts of London and coastal towns in the South, with severe and multiple social and economic problems. These long-term transitions and pressures have not been the outcomes of smooth and incremental processes, however, but instead have involved the effects of several destabilizing shocks and disturbances. Over the past four decades, in what seems to have become an era of heightened economic turbulence and instability throughout the global economy, the UK has been repeatedly disrupted by major shocks, including the major recessions of 1980–83, 1990–93 and 2008–10, and now the unfolding consequences of the UK's exit from the European Union (EU), and the impact of the Covid-19 pandemic.

Economists have usually treated recessionary and similar shocks as temporary interruptions to an economy's long-run growth path which otherwise remains unchanged. In other words, shocks are assumed to have only transient downward impacts, and interest focuses on how quickly the economy "bounces back" to its long-run trajectory (typically assumed to be its "full employment growth ceiling"). Yet there is evidence that shocks may actually have longer lasting and even permanent effects. Economies that experience more severe, or more protracted, or more frequent shocks tend to have lower long-run growth rates than economies less so effected by shocks.[2] This raises the important question of whether the same relationship might apply to regional, urban and local economies within a country. More specifically, to what extent has the divergent growth of regions, cities and towns across the UK been due to the differential capacity of places to recover from major shocks? What underpins and accounts for their differential resilience to such disruptions? Answers to these questions are fundamentally important in considering the challenges faced by "left behind places" and the "levelling up" agenda. The impact of economic shocks and resilience and adaptive capacity of places to withstand, cope with and prepare for future disruptions are geographically differentiated.

4.2 THE NOTION OF LOCAL ECONOMIC RESILIENCE

Over the past decade or so, the notion of "resilience" has attracted prominent attention from academics across numerous disciplines and amongst policymakers. Considerable interest has

Regional Studies Policy Impact Books

https://doi.org/10.1080/2578711X.2021.1992170

come to be focused on the ability of people, organizations, communities, economies, public services and infrastructures to maintain their core purpose and integrity in the face of what seems to be a "new normal" of constant disruption, of frequently recurring shocks, some of historic proportions. This new emphasis on "resilience" directs attention to issues of adaptabil-ity and agility in response to shocks, rapid change and uncertainty, and to how such features can be fostered to yield what some have called the "resilience dividend" (Box 4.1).

This idea of resilience is of considerable potential importance for understanding the economic growth paths of regions, cities and localities.[4] Resilience in this context is the capacity of a local economy to recover successfully from a disruptive shock, for example, the closure of a local major employer, the impact of a national recession, the sudden collapse of that economy's major export markets, the rupture caused by a global economic crisis or some other major disturbance (Box 4.2).

There are essentially three aspects to local resilience: a locality's risk of shocks (its vulnerability or exposure), its resistance to shocks (how far it is affected), and its recoverability (not just how quickly and how far it "bounces back" to its pre-shock path, but whether it "bounces forward" to a "better" or more desirable path, for example, at higher levels of output and/or employ-ment and which is more productive, sustainable and socially inclusive) (Figure 4.1).

Figure 4.1 Shocks, resilience and local economic development paths

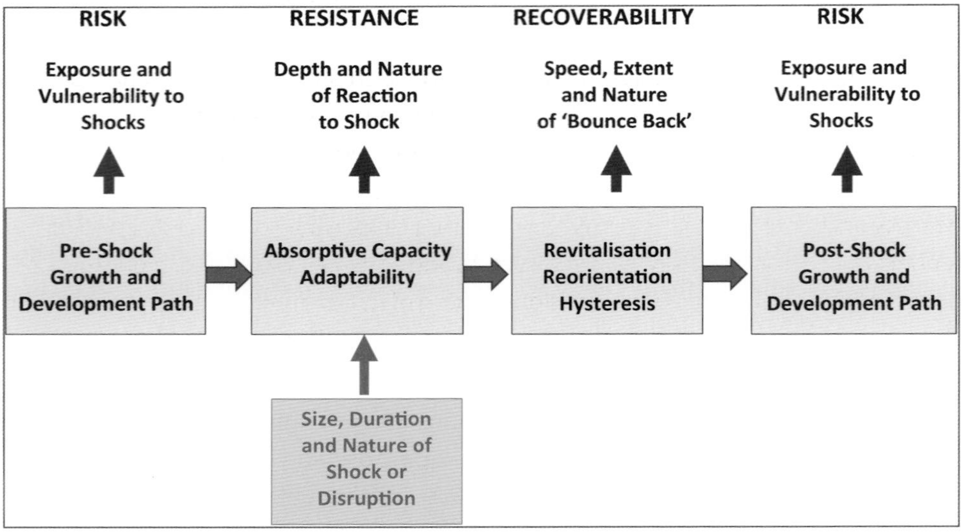

Source: Adapted from Martin and Sunley.[6]

Both a locality's risk and resistance will depend, in part at least, on the form and nature of its pre-shock growth path, on its economic and business structures, its supply chain connections and dependencies, its export mix, its skill base, its entrepreneurial culture, and perhaps even its local institutional and governance arrangements. The absorptive capacity and adaptability of these features will shape the locality's resistance to the shock, and the nature of its recoverability from it, but in the process may undergo reorientation and reconfiguration, so that recovery itself involves changes to the locality's growth path, and its vulnerability to future shocks.

Recoverability, then, takes on particular importance since it can assume different forms. Most worrying is the case where a shock erodes so much of a locality's productive and employment base (through closures of firms and destruction of jobs), that it emerges on a growth path inferior to and lower than its pre-shock path. In this instance, it may take a considerable time even to recover to its pre-shock level of activity—a case of negative hysteresis. At the other extreme, the creative aspects of a shock might outweigh the destructive, for example, where the shock stimulates new activities and jobs, and resources are redeployed in more productive and innovative ways, so that the locality emerges on a higher and faster growth path than its pre-shock one—a case of positive hysteresis. Clearly, there are likely to be numerous variations between these extremes. The key point is that differential recoverability across places can shape differences in their long-run growth and developmental paths.

In many instances, where a growth path is weak the effect of a recession is to reinforce that loss of momentum through negative hysteresis. Without intervention, places with depressed economies have been found to suffer an erosion of the capacities needed to sustain resilience. A good example is the recession of the early 1980s which was felt most strongly in Britain's struggling manufacturing heartlands.[7] The collapse of employment was so severe in Northern regions that their working-age employment rates did not recover for several decades until the late 2000s.[8] Many of the local areas that suffered the largest adverse shocks in the 1970s and 1980s remain amongst the most deprived in 2015.[9] Of course, the consequences of shocks and recessions inevitably involve an element of unpredictability and longer term processes do not entirely determine resilience to a recession. The impacts also depend on the specific origins and impacts of the recession, as different downturns have different causes and chronologies, and may have a differential effect across different industry sectors and activities. Moreover, economic resilience is also fundamentally shaped by the decision-making of national and local economic and political actors, and by whether these decisions accentuate or ameliorate the impacts of the shock.[10]

4.3 ECONOMIC RESILIENCE ACROSS UK LOCALITIES

Previous research on UK, US and European regions and cities has revealed significant differences in resilience between places, and the potential implications for understanding why some places become "left behind".[11] Table 4.1 shows the correlations between the resistance and recovery of local employment across the 370 UK local authority districts (LADs) association with the four recessions of 1974–76, 1980–83, 1990–93 and 2008–10. Several features stand out. In the recessions of 1974–76 and 1980–83, localities that were more resistant to the shock also tended to recover faster from it. In both cases, Northern localities tended to be the least resistant to the downturns, while Southern localities tended to have the fastest recovery

Table 4.1 Correlations between resistance and recovery in employment across 370 local authority districts (LADs), 1974–2018

	Recession 1974–76	Recovery 1976–80	Recession 1980–83	Recovery 1983–90	Recession 1990–93	Recovery 1993–2008	Recession 2008–10	Recovery 2010–18
1974–76	1.00	0.340*	0.412*					
1976–80		1.00	0.398*	0.271*				
1980–83			1.00	0.241*	−0.030			
1983–90				1.00	−0.043	0.246*		
1990–93					1.00	−0.085	−0.027	
1993–2008						1.00	−0.079	0.245*
2008–10							1.00	−0.250*
2010–18								1.00

Note: Resistance and recoverability of a locality are defined as: (actual % change in a locality–expected % change in the locality)/modulus (expected % change in the locality), where the expected % change is set equal to the actual national % change.*Correlation is statistically significant at the 5% level.

https://doi.org/10.1080/2578711X.2021.1992170

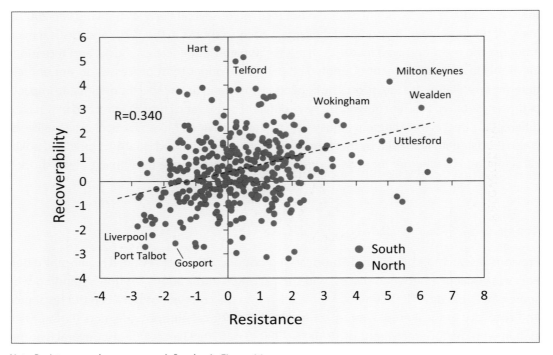

Note: Resistance and recovery are defined as in Figure 4.1.

(Figure 4.2). But in the last two recessionary shocks, of 1990–93 and 2008–10, that relationship has disappeared, and it now seems that localities that are least resistant may not in fact have the lowest recoverability, though a high proportion of Southern localities still exhibited greater recoverability (Figure 4.3). In addition, the relationship between the strength of recovery and resistance to the next shock has changed from being positive to negative. Reinforcing the greater level of unpredictability involved, recoverability from a shock is no longer a guide to the geographies of resistance to the next shock.

This situation seems to be a result of the fact that geographical incidence of shocks has changed. This is not surprising, given that the causes of recessions and other shocks varies, one to another, and that local economies themselves have been evolving and changing over time (not least shifting their employment structures away from manufacturing to services), thus altering their vulnerability and reaction to successive shocks when these occur. It means, however, that it has become much less predictable as to how such shocks will now play out across the UK's cities, regions and towns. However, the local pattern of recoverability has shown more stability over time: the pattern of recoverability across successive shocks is positive, with a tendency for the localities that recovered faster than the national economy in one recession also to recover faster in the next. This is important, since it suggests that this aspect

https://doi.org/10.1080/2578711X.2021.1992170

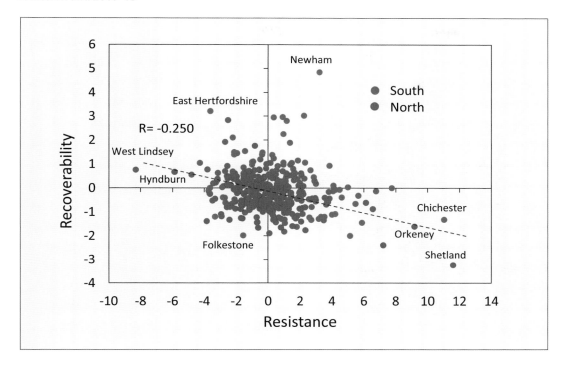

of local economic resilience—the degree of relative recoverability from recessions—has contributed to the widening of spatial inequalities in economic growth across localities in the UK, and as a result is an integral part of the "left behind" problem.

Notwithstanding these developments, over the past four major recessions recoverability has tended to decline with increasing distance of cities from London.[12] Unsurprisingly, the recent resilience of London to the recession of 2008–10 has been the subject of some investigation which has tried to understand the conjunction of long-term shifts with short-term responses. London has always been relatively resilient in terms of its recoverability from recessions. But its recoverability has increased markedly since the recession of the early 1990s, in part because of its strong employment growth in many service sectors, not just knowledge-intensive business services (KIBS) activities, but also low-wage and low-skilled services.[13]

London emerged from the 2008–10 recession with rapid employment growth: it accounted for more than 1.1 million of the 3.4 million new jobs created in the national economy over that period. Despite warnings that it would be very badly hit by the global financial crisis and the recession this produced, London escaped remarkably unscathed: it proved much more resilient than most other major cities in the UK.[14] The picture was the same for output: compared with the core cities, London's recovery stood out (Figure 4.4). What is also striking is that in

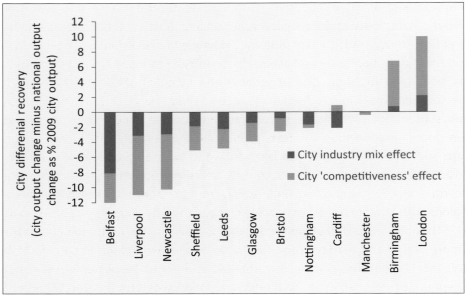

Note: Shift–share components of the percentage change in city output minus the Great Britain national change. The analysis is based on 45 sectors of activity. For further discussion of the analysis, see Martin and Gardiner.[15]

London, as in most of the core cities, industry mix contributed less than city "competitiveness" to output recovery.

The sense of grievance and emergent geography of discontent generated by the weaker and slower recovery seen in many Northern towns and cities was intensified by public sector austerity and cuts to public employment, services, and community organizations and facilities. The largest cutbacks to public spending occurred in many already peripheral and disadvantaged regions that had previously received relatively higher levels of redistributive transfers of resources.[16] As the preceding chapters demonstrate, this evolving situation has underpinned the geographically uneven development in the UK since the 2008 crash.

4.4 THE EMERGING IMPLICATIONS OF BREXIT AND THE PANDEMIC SHOCKS

The importance of understanding the causes and consequences of uneven resilience has assumed heightened relevance in the context of two current profound shocks to the British economy, namely the country's departure from the EU (Brexit) and the consequences of the Covid-19 pandemic. A significant amount has already been written about the likely effects of

Brexit on the geographical inequalities and "left-behind" places, but much of this has been speculative. At the time of writing, we do not have data on the longer term effects on trade, labour movements, regional and research funding, service and finance industry exports, and foreign direct investment and associated supply chains. Much of this work has estimated the effects of heightened trade friction with the EU Single Market on industry sectors and then mapped the distribution of sectors across the country to estimate the exposure of different regions. An early example argued that negative effect would be felt most strongly in London and the Southern region and urban areas, due to their specialization in service exports.[17] However, subsequent work concludes that Brexit is on course to increase the challenges faced by many poorer and "left behind" areas, reinforcing their already challenging predicament. Northern and Western regions have been found to be more vulnerable to Brexit-related trade risks.[18] Using a detailed input–output database to trace effects on supply chains and production, Thissen et al. find that regions way from London, and especially medium-sized city-regions such as Manchester, Liverpool and Leeds, will be adversely affected to a greater degree.[19] They also suggest that weaker local economies within each regional economy will suffer more. Martin and Gardiner urge caution when estimating local Brexit effects, but also conclude that London is likely to be least effected by the post-Brexit trading realities, though much depends on continuing negotiations over market access for financial services.[20]

Discerning the consequences and costs of Brexit has, of course, been greatly complicated by the fact that they have begun to materialize at the same time as the unprecedented economic consequences of the current global Covid-19 pandemic. While the effects of the pandemic continue to unfold and remain to be fully documented, there is growing evidence that it has intensified the pre-existing trend to geographical divergence by worsening the problems of low-income regions, and of disadvantaged and vulnerable communities. In many ways, the pandemic has made the challenge of "levelling up" even more difficult by exacerbating many existing inequalities.[21] Put simply, the structural processes described in this chapter have undermined the resilience of "left behind" places to the pandemic. Many relatively poor urban areas are marked by a greater prevalence of poor health and underlying conditions that have aggravated the grip and consequences of the virus. Many such communities have compound problems of vulnerability and a lack of social resources. Labour market conditions have strongly shaped vulnerability and resilience.[22] Lower skilled workers in service occupations have been much more exposed to the disease as they have been unable to work from home, and this has intensified the spread and persistence of Covid-19 in poorer communities. The sectors that have been most negatively impacted are accommodation and food, arts and entertainment, wholesale trades and retail, transport and construction.[23] All these sectors are heavily reliant on low-wage labour. Allas et al., for example, found that 50% of the jobs negatively impacted by the pandemic in the UK, through layoffs, furloughs and reductions in hours, were paid less than £10 an hour.[24] The heaviest economic toll has thus been felt by younger and low-income workers and ethnic minorities.[25]

It is no surprise that local areas with weaker low skill economies in the North West, Scotland and Midlands, and in cities such as Birmingham, Hull and Blackpool, have been most strongly impacted. Houston finds that the growth in unemployment during the recession has been related to prior levels of unemployment, and that seaside towns and coastal areas reliant on tourism, particularly areas of Cornwall, have also been highly vulnerable in economic terms.[26] There is mounting evidence that the pandemic shock has added a further layer of distress to already deprived communities in the Midlands and North. In addition, the ongoing disruption has added a new patchwork dimension by strongly affecting some parts of the South that are heavily dependent on travel and tourism, such as the major airport locations of Crawley, Slough and Luton.[27] At present, little is known about the strength of recovery from the pandemic shock across the country. There is some evidence that the consumer footfall in big cities has been slower to recover that those in smaller and provincial cities. Consumer spending has recovered most strongly in the Southern Home Counties around London. However, it will be some time before the recovery patterns become clearer.

4.5 CONCLUSIONS: RESILIENCE AND RECOVERY

The unprecedented impacts of the pandemic have triggered a debate in economic geography about whether this is a turning point that signals a decline in the economic prospects of cities as activity will shift away from dense urban areas. Much of this debate has argued that this is unlikely because face-to-face interaction remains essential for tacit knowledge exchange, creativity and innovation. Work has somewhat quickly concluded that the age of the "superstar" global and innovation hotspot cities will continue.[28] However, there is much more profound uncertainty about the majority of cities, and this interpretation underestimates some of the national and subnational variability in outcomes. Given the employment trends documented in this chapter, there are grounds for thinking that the pandemic will intensify the problems of cities and formerly industrial large towns.

Recall that in Chapters 2 and 3 we have argued that there are two fundamental and interconnected modes of growth in post-industrial capital: one that is agglomerated and focused on high-knowledge activities; and one which is more dispersed across different types of settlement and involves a range of lower skill sectors. There are reasons to expect that the pandemic consequences will affect both these forms of growth. While the existing literature may be correct to suggest that the need for clustering and proximity in the first mode will be as important as before, the key question about this type of growth is how much employment it will generate and whether wealth and jobs will diffuse from "hotspots" into surrounding areas. As we have seen, much of this growth has produced considerable wealth, output and innovation, but it has often not spread benefits throughout urban communities by generating sufficient

 https://doi.org/10.1080/2578711X.2021.1992170

jobs for their populations. The pandemic may make this type of concentrated growth even less beneficial for employment as virtual and hybrid working become normalized.

Second, in a relatively small country such as Britain, it is highly likely that the pandemic will reinforce the long-term trends towards an urban–rural shift which has been driven by some deep-rooted locational preferences. Hybrid and digital working, plus an unwillingness to return to everyday lengthy commuting, are bound to further intensify the dispersion of much activity to suburban regions and to smaller cities and towns. The longer it takes to exit the pandemic, the stronger this effect is likely to be.[29] To some degree, such changes may represent an opportunity for "levelling up", although as we have seen in Chapter 3, this spread has been highly selective, and has discriminated between places according to the quality of their living and working environments. Together these trends are likely to reinforce the huge economic challenges faced by large urban areas, especially in the North, and to intensify London's internal inequality. To argue that these cities and their satellite towns will rapidly bounce back, borne by a returning wave of urban and big city resurgence, misreads the post-industrial trends seen over the past 40 years and effectively represents somewhat wishful thinking.

NOTES

[1] Zolli A and Healy AM (2012) *Resilience: Why Things Bounce Back*. London: Headline, at book cover.

[2] Cerra V and Saxena S (2008) Growth dynamics: The myth of recovery. *American Economic Review*, 98: 439–457; Cerra V, Panizza U and Saxena S (2009) *International Evidence on Recovery from Recessions* (Working Paper No. 09/183). Washington, DC: International Monetary Fund (IMF).

[3] Rodin J (2015) *The Resilience Dividend: Managing Disruption, Avoiding Disaster and Growing Stronger in an Unpredictable World*, pp. 3–4. London: Profile.

[4] For example, see Christopherson S, Michie J and Tyler P (2010) Regional resilience; theoretical and empirical perspectives. *Cambridge Journal of Regions, Economy and Society*, 3: 3–10; Martin RL (2012) Regional economic resilience, hysteresis and recessionary shocks. *Journal of Economic Geography*, 12: 1–32; Doran J and Fingleton B (2013) US metropolitan resilience: Insights from dynamic spatial panel estimation. Paper presented at the Annual Conference of the Regional Science Association International, University of Cambridge, Cambridge, UK, 22 August; Martin RL (2018) Towards an economic geography of resilience. In Clark GL, Feldman MA, Gertler M and Wojcik D (eds.), *New Handbook of Economic Geography*, pp. 839–864. Oxford: Oxford University Press; Martin RL and Sunley P (2015) On the notion of regional economic resilience; Conceptualization and explanation. *Journal of Economic Geography*, 15: 1–42; Martin RL and Sunley P (2020) Regional economic resilience: Evolution and evaluation. In G Bristow and A Healy (eds.), *Handbook on Regional Economic Resilience*, pp. 10–35. Cheltenham: Edward Elgar; Martin RL and Gardiner B (2019) The resilience of cities to economic shocks: A tale of four recessions (and the challenge of Brexit). *Papers in Regional Science*, 98(4): 1801–1832; Martin RL and Gardiner B (2021) The resilience of Britain's core cities to the great

recession (with implications for the Covid recessionary shock). In R Wink (ed.), *Resilience for Regions, Organisations and Management*, pp. 57–89. Amsterdam: Springer; Bristow G and Healy A (eds.) (2020) *Handbook on Regional Economic Resilience*. Cheltenham: Edward Elgar; and Sensier M and Devine F (2020) Understanding regional economic performance and resilience in the UK: Trends since the global financial crisis. *National Institute Economic Review*, 253: R18–R28.

[5] Martin and Sunley (2020), p. 15, see Reference 4.

[6] Martin and Sunley (2020), see Reference 4.

[7] Martin and Gardiner (2019, 2021), see Reference 4.

[8] Rowthorn RE (2010) Combined and uneven development: Reflections on the North–South divide. *Spatial Economic Analysis*, 5: 363–388.

[9] Rice P and Venables A (2021) The persistent consequences of adverse shocks: How the 1970s shaped UK regional inequality. *Oxford Review of Economic Policy*, 37: 132–151.

[10] Martin and Sunley (2020), see Reference 4.

[11] Martin (2012); Martin and Sunley (2015); Martin and Gardiner (2019); Sensier and Devine (2020), see Reference 4.

[12] Martin and Gardiner (2019), see Reference 4.

[13] Martin and Gardiner (2021), see Reference 4.

[14] Overman H (2011) *How Did London Get Away With It?* London: Spatial Economics Research Centre. http://spatial-economics.blogspot.co.uk/2011/01/how-did-london-get-away-with-it.html/.

[15] Martin and Gardiner (2021), see Reference 4.

[16] Gray M and Barford A (2018) The depths of the cuts: The uneven geography of local government austerity. *Cambridge Journal of Regions, Economy and Society*, 11: 541–563.

[17] Dhingra S, Machin S and Overman H (2017) Local economic effects of Brexit. *National Institute Economic Review*, 242(1): R24–R36.

[18] Chen W, Los B, McCann P, Ortega-Argilés R, Thisssen M and Van Ort F (2017) The continental divide? Economic exposure to Brexit in regions and countries on both sides of the Channel. *Papers in Regional Science*, 97(1): 25–54.

[19] Thissen M, Van Ort F, McCann P, Ortega-Argilés R and Husby T (2020) The implications of Brexit for UK and EU regional competitiveness. *Economic Geography*, 96: 397–421.

[20] Martin and Gardiner (2019), see Reference 4.

[21] Oxford Consultants for Social Inclusion (OCSI) (2020) *Communities at Risk: The Early Impact of COVID-19 on 'Left Behind' Neighbourhoods: A Data Dive for the All-Party Parliamentary Group for Left Behind Neighbourhoods*. appg-leftbehindneighbourhoods.org.uk; Blundell R, Costa Dias M and Joyce R (2020) COVID-19 and inequalities. *Fiscal Studies*, 41: 291–319.

[22] Davenport A, Farquharson C, Rsael I, Sibieta L and Stoye G (2020) *The Geography of the COVID-19 Crisis in England*. London: Institute for Fiscal Studies (IFS).

[23] Petrie K and Norman A (2020) *Assessing the Economic Implications of Coronavirus and Brexit*. London: Social Market Foundation.

[24] Allas T, Canal M and Hunt V (2020) *COVID-19 in the United Kingdom: Assessing Jobs at Risk and the Impact on People and Places*. London: Public Sector Practice, McKinsey & Co.

[25] Powell A and Francis-Devine B (2021) *Coronavirus: Impact on the Labour Market* (CBP8898). London: House of Commons Library.

[26] Houston D (2020) Local resistance to rising unemployment in the context of the COVID-19 mitigation policies across Great Britain. *Regional Science Policy and Practice*, 12(6): 1189–1209.

[27] Davenport A et al. (2020), see Reference 22.

[28] Hendrikson C and Muro M (2020) *Will COVID-19 Rebalance America's Uneven Economic Geography? Don't Bet On It* (Brookings Metro's COVID-19 Analysis). Washington, DC: Brookings Institution.

[29] Nathan M and Overman H (2020) Will coronavirus cause a big city exodus? *EPB: Urban Analytics and City Science*, 47: 1537–1542.

5. LEARNING FROM PAST POLICIES FOR "LEVELLING UP" AND "LEFT BEHIND PLACES" IN THE UK

Keywords: left behind places, levelling up, types of spatial policy, limited impact in the past, policy churn, inadequate funding

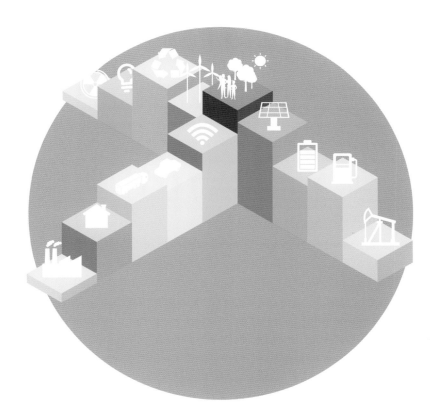

> *Despite all the disagreement surrounding the analysis of the "regional problem", the one thing upon which the academic and political participants in the current regional policy debate are agreed upon, is that the policies that began life in 1945–7 are inadequate to the enormous task of ameliorating the condition of depressed areas.*[1]

5.1 LEARNING FROM THE PAST

The longstanding scale and nature of the problems confronting "left behind places" present a stark challenge to the "levelling up" agenda and institutional and policy responses in the UK. A key concern is that despite over 90 years of local, regional and urban policies of various kinds, geographical inequalities have not only persisted but also, as we have seen in Chapters 2 and 3, intensified in recent decades. Central questions must be:

- Why have past policies not proved more effective in reducing these inequalities?

- Were past policies not up to the task?

- Were they even flawed in certain key aspects?

- Are the sort of policies followed in the past no longer appropriate for the scale and nature of the "levelling up" and "left behind" problem we face today?

Addressing such questions is important for at least two reasons: (1) because of the lessons to be learned about why in the UK (and indeed elsewhere) past policies have failed to have a significant lasting impact; and (2) because in recent years the very notion of "spatial" economic policy has become the subject of lively discussion and debate among academics and policymakers.[2] In much discourse, reference is now less to the notions of "regional policy" or "urban policy" and increasingly to the idea of "place-based policy". The argument seems to be that past regional policies have had limited impact in reviving economically lagging areas because they have been insufficiently "place-based".[3] The implication is that only the latter offers any real prospect of redressing geographical inequalities in economic prosperity and performance.

In addressing the UK government's ambition of "levelling up" the UK, and how that task might best be achieved, it is important to first assess the veracity of such claims. What is actually meant by the notion of "place-based" policy? Is it the case that past local, regional and urban policies in the UK have not been sufficiently "place based"? We argue that while there is certainly some validity to this charge, there are other fundamental reasons why past spatial economic policies have not produced the impacts hoped for. And we also argue that the very idea of "place-based policy" is itself not straightforward, nor of itself the panacea some might claim. A "place-based" approach to local economic policy intervention may be necessary, but of itself is unlikely to be sufficient.

https://doi.org/10.1080/2578711X.2021.1992171

5.2 DISTINGUISHING SPATIAL POLICIES

Underpinned by the "New Urban Economics" and "New Economic Geography" thinking,[4] economic development policy has been marked by the rise of people-based, territorially universal and "spatially blind" approaches in the wake of the 2008 financial crisis. Reprising a longstanding debate,[5] the case for more explicitly "place-based" policies was reasserted in response.[6] What has been missing is a clearer specification of the different kinds of "place-based" policy within this category, reflections upon its potentials and limitations, and identification of the other types of spatial policy that are important in addressing geographical inequalities namely spatially sensitive policies.

Three main kinds of spatial policies can be distinguished (Table 5.1). The first is based on the *spatial targeting* of policies to specified and selected areas in order to boost their economic development. This approach is typically more top down and centralized in its design and roll-out by national governments. The geographical scale of areas varies from regions to more localized areas. Examples include various types of area-based initiatives such as enterprise zones in the UK and opportunity zones in the United States.[7] Even former staunch advocates of people-based and spatially blind policies now propose such spatially targeted policies to address spatial inequalities in economic prosperity and social conditions.[8] Typical policy instruments include financial incentives, job subsidies, tax breaks, planning rule relaxations and infrastructural provision available within the spatially delimited areas.

In seeking to create employment opportunities, this kind of targeted spatial policy approach is actually often more people-focused rather than explicitly area-based in its goals. It aims

Table 5.1 Three types of spatial policy

Type of spatial policy	Main characteristics
Spatially targeted	Typically "top-down" policies designed by central government (or authority) and administered in undifferentiated form in specifically targeted "development" or "assisted" places (regions or localities) designated on the basis of key indicators of economic and social disadvantage. Little or no discretion over policy design or implementation by authorities or actors at the regional or local levels
Place sensitive	Policies that are differentiated to some extent by "type" of designated place (region or locality) and thereby intended to be sensitive to the development or other problems shared by that particular "type" or "club" of assisted regions or localities. Policies typically designed by central government (or authority), that is, "top down", although may contain some element of local discretion or autonomy over precise policy mix and implementation
Place based	Policies and strategies designed and implemented by a place's local authority and other local policy actors and institutions, intended to respond to the specific problems and potentialities of that particular place, involving collaboration with various local stakeholders, and combining local sources of funding (e.g., from local business, property or income taxes) with central government or other authority funding streams. Democratically accountable to local voters.

Source: Authors' own elaboration.

to improve opportunities for people rather than reduce spatial disparities between places.[9] Resource allocation is typically determined through inter-area competition with the aim of fostering innovation, leveraging in local resources, strengthening bids, and building local collaboration and partnerships. Such initiatives suffer from displacement and time-limited effects tied to the duration of their incentives.[10] They are also vulnerable to changing national levels of funding and wasteful effort and duplication by local actors in bidding for relatively small-scale and short-term initiatives.

A second but as yet somewhat unrecognized approach is "place-sensitive" policy. This perspective classifies different types of areas into "regional clubs" with shared characteristics based on their level of development, ranges of per capita personal incomes or other such indicators.[11] This "place-sensitive distributed development policy" is then advocated to address the specific issues of each type of place. A version of this approach, though not explicitly advanced under the terminology of "place-sensitive" policy, characterized UK regional policy of selective assistance during the 1970s and 1980s, when the geographical areas selected as eligible for aid were divided into five groups, defined by the severity of their employment and related problems, with different levels of capital grants and other forms of business assistance (special development areas, development areas, intermediate areas, derelict land clearance areas, and special measures for Northern Ireland). Developed to date at the regional scale, the "place-sensitive" approach to spatial policy provides a degree of tailoring to the needs of different types of places. However, it remains relatively more top down than bottom up, operates at a broader level of principles rather than specific policies, and says little about how such place-sensitive policies and their economic, social and/or environmental aims should be decided.

The third type of spatial policy is more "place based" and led by actors in places in a bottom-up way. It is defined as more sensitive to place and better able to address persistent inefficiencies and spatial inequalities by tailoring public goods and services to particular local, regional and urban contexts, problems and potentialities.[12] Policy is designed with explicit consideration of geographical setting and context because it is understood that "space matters and shapes the potential for development not only of territories, but, through externalities, of the individuals who live in them".[13]

This "place-based" approach has been further developed to include several distinguishing features.[14] These have been defined as comprising sensitivity to local context and the identification and customization of policy to local opportunities, the autonomy and discretion for local stakeholders to design and implement policies, and effective and inclusive local leadership, decision-making and collaboration. There should also be coordination, vertically and horizontally, across and between relevant institutions at different spatial levels, and sufficient resources appropriate to the scale of the policy goals. The latter should be oriented towards the sustainability of development outcomes and building upon and learning from effective policies that

https://doi.org/10.1080/2578711X.2019.1547489

> **Box 5.1   Key determinants of success in "place-based' policy"**
>
> - Develop an explicit focus on place and work to make use of the full set of opportunities and resources in that locality
> - Foster an engagement with local institutions to achieve the mission of each place-based policy
> - Focus on governance, accepting the need to create robust, sustainable and transparent processes, and acknowledging the key role of erudite and charismatic local leaders
> - Emphasize value creation and the local capture of value in order to generate opportunities in the short, medium and long terms
> - Acknowledge the need to consider the performance of places over a long time frame
> - Prioritize the assistance to those individuals and groups for whom adjustment processes are most challenging
> - Accept that there is an emotional dimension to questions of place and the future of places which may especially evident in periods of rapid change - such as disruptions to local industries—but is present in all circumstances
> - Incorporate outcome and output measures—qualitative and quantitative—early in the implementation of place-based initiatives in order to drive achievement
> - Avoid faltering expectations and a cycle of disillusionment by having demonstrable significant achievements built into the programme design. These can be short term, long term or developmental and they need to be communicated to all stakeholders
>
> *Source*: Beer et al.[16]

have succeeded elsewhere.[15] Key "success" factors of place-based policy have been codified in broad terms (Box 5.1).

Such a "place-based" approach is, however, founded on a relatively narrow evidence base concerning its effectiveness and timescales.[17] It raises questions about whether the framework encourages mimicry of strategies among areas, rather than the development of distinctive place-specific approaches. There is also the danger that this type of policy framework will favour those places that are already advantaged in relation to policymaking capacity and resources. This issue has been a specific concern with "Smart Specialisation" strategies.[18] The approach also relies on key factors often outside the control of local stakeholders. Supportive institutional and policy frameworks are needed at the national and even international levels, for example, through coordination and integration of policies and appropriate funding. It is also crucially dependent upon the quality and capacity of local leaderships in developing and implementing a long-term vision and strategic policy programmes to achieve it.

Distinguishing the different kinds, roles, and relative advantages and limitations of these three spatial policy approaches is important in formulating the response to "left behind" places as part of any "levelling up" agenda in the UK. Clearer understanding is needed of the different kinds of spatially targeted, "place-sensitive" and "place-based" polices and their interrelations, as well as their connection, alignment and coordination with ostensibly more "spatially blind" national policies and expenditures.

5.3 NINE DECADES OF THE UK SPATIAL POLICY

The UK has had a long history in local, regional and urban policies of various kinds. Indeed, it has been a pioneer and influential internationally in leading experiments in spatial policy.[19] The first "experiments" in official spatial policy date to the Industrial Transference Act 1928, under which certain measures and incentives were introduced to encourage unemployed workers to move out of depressed coalmining and heavy industrial areas and sites of discontent and social protest in Northern Britain to jobs and training in the Southern half of the country: a policy of "taking workers to the work". This was followed by the Special Areas Act 1934, by which capital incentives were offered in those same areas to entice firms to locate and expand there: a policy of "taking work to the workers". This latter approach, endorsed by the famous Barlow Commission Report of 1940, which argued for a spatial rebalancing of the economy away from London,[20] was to provide the basic underlying cornerstone of the "redistributive" or "diversionary" style of regional policy that was followed in the post-war period, at least up to the end of the 1970s. Also over this period, urban-focused policies were developed, most often with a focus on regenerating the built environment and economic prospects in the inner areas of major cities across the UK, including parts of London. Of course, various specific measures and changes were made to both regional and urban policy over the decades. We cannot describe all of them here. Instead, their broad features, and the phases in their evolution, are summarized in Tables 5.2 and 5.3.

Across this outline history, the key characteristics are: shifting aims between economic and/or social goals, especially in relation to jobs and their geographical availability and location; evolving rationales for intervention from achieving social and spatial equity to addressing market failures and promoting economic efficiency; and changing and multiple geographies and scales, with frequent redrawing of the maps of areas eligible for policy support. There have also been uneven connections and coordination between spatial economic and other spatial policies, including housing and regeneration, as well as temporally punctuated "policy-on" and "policy-off" episodes, determined by different degrees of government financial resource devoted to their pursuit. The policy instruments of spatially targeted incentives and controls to influence the geography of capital investment and labour recruitment have also varied over time, typically with changes in government. Another notable feature has been shifting resource allocation mechanisms, from mandatory to approaches based on sectorally focused support for manufacturing and services towards more horizontal, supply-side measures focused on supporting enterprise, innovation, technological upgrading and skills.

https://doi.org/10.1080/2578711X.2019.1547489

Table 5.2 The evolution of the UK regional policy: main features

	1928–39	1945–79	1979–97	1997–2010	2010–present
Geographical focus	Economically depressed "assisted areas" of coalfields and heavy industry, in North East and North West England, the Glasgow region and South Wales	Gradual expansion southwards of "development areas" to encompass over 42% of the UK working population	Rolling back of "development areas" to produce a more spatially fragmented map of localities and "districts" eligible for aid covering 20% of the working population	All standard regions of the UK, including London	System of 38 local enterprise partnership (LEP) areas in England. Devolved nations (Scotland, Wales, Northern Ireland) treated separately
Interpretation of problem regions ("left behind" places')	As a social problem of the unemployed in areas worst hit by recessions	Keynesian: economic depression due to lack of demand in local industries	Neo-classical: local supply-side inadequacies and failures	Endogenous growth theory: lack of local core assets and competencies	Endogenous growth theory: poor local skills, poor connectivity and lack of infrastructure
Key aims of policy	To reduce unemployment and social unrest in "assisted areas"	To produce a better spatial distribution (balance) of industry and employment	To promote enterprise and wage flexibility in the "development areas"	To promote local productivity and competitiveness	To promote local productivity. Spatially rebalancing the economy
Main Instruments/ policies	Transferring labour out of depressed areas and an inducement to firms to move to and create jobs in those areas	Capital grants in "development areas" combined with industrial controls on new investment in prosperous South and East	Reduction in grants. Abolition of industrial controls. Focus on wage flexibility. Creation of enterprise zones	Creation of a nationwide system of regional development agencies (RDAs) charged with drawing up development strategies	RDAs abolished. New nationwide system of LEPs and local industrial strategies. Various central initiatives competed for by local authorities (Local Growth Fund, Growing Places Fund, etc.)
Institutional structures	Top-down policies by central government departments	Top-down policies by central government departments	Top-down policies by central government departments	More bottom-up system of policymaking involving elements of devolution and decentralization to regional and local levels	Further devolution and decentralization of policy to local levels (LEPs and new combined authorities)
Forms of spatial policy	Spatially targeted	Spatially targeted	Spatially targeted with some place-sensitive elements	Spatially targeted with some place-sensitive and place-based elements	Spatially targeted with some place-sensitive and place-based elements

Sources: Authors' own elaboration of McCrone and Parsons.[21]

Table 5.3 The evolution of urban policy: main features

	1945–68	1968–79	1979–97	1997–2010	2010–present
Geographical focus	Large urban areas, particularly conurbations	Selected urban authorities. Addressing specific areas of social need in inner cities	Local authorities, inner cities and individual neighbourhoods areas	Local authorities and designated/ nominated areas and neighbourhoods	System of 38 local enterprise partnership (LEP) areas. Local authorities/ combined authorities
Interpretation of "problem" urban areas	As a social problem of overcrowding, poor living conditions and congestion	Initially as a social problem, later emphasis is shifted to addressing economic problems caused by de-industrializa- tion	Neo-classical: local supply-side inadequacies and failures, particularly in urban land and property and labour markets	Lack of core assets and competencies, poor housing and inadequate built environment	Endogenous growth theory: poor local skills, poor connectiv- ity, lack of infrastructure
Key aims of policy	Decentralization of activity from urban areas and improvement of living conditions	To improve social welfare particularly relating to education, housing and health	To promote and stimulate enterprise and market flexibility in urban land, property and labour markets	To reduce social exclusion, promote local productivity, competitiveness and employability	To promote growth of local productivity and competitiveness
Main instruments/ policies	New towns and overspill policies. Substantial programme of urban renewal, particularly housing related	Urban pro- gramme (1968)	Urban develop- ment corpora- tions, enterprise zones, task forces, city action teams, city challenge and single regeneration budget	National strategy for neighbour- hood renewal, creation of a social exclusion unit. New Deal for Communities. Local strategic partnerships	Various central initiatives competed for by local authorities (City Deals, Local Growth Fund, Growing Places Fund, etc).
Institutional structures	Top-down policies by central government departments and implemented by development corporations and local authorities	Top-down policies by central govern- ment departments	Top-down policies by central government departments, bid for local by authorities. Urban development corporations. Area-based initiatives	Extension of area-based initiatives. Some policymaking involving elements of devolution and decentralization to local levels. Centrally funded	Further elements of devolution of centrally funded policy to local authorities, LEPs and new combined authorities
Forms of spatial policy	Spatially targeted	Spatially targeted	Spatially targeted with some place-sensitive elements	Spatially targeted with some place-sensitive and place-based elements	Spatially targeted with some place-sensitive and place-based elements

https://doi.org/10.1080/2578711X.2019.1547489

Throughout its history, UK regional policy has been typically treated as an adjunct to national macro-economic policy, not as integral to it, and as such a ready target for cuts if public spending were deemed to be too high, or for "rolling back" if a less committed government were elected.[22] At the same time, it has rarely been properly acknowledged by UK governments that ostensibly "spatially blind" national macro-economic policies often have spatially differentiated effects, sometimes working with, sometimes against, specifically regional and urban policies.[23]

A summative assessment can be provided of past policies in the UK in relation to the key features of the different kinds of spatial policy approach—the more spatially targeted, top-down version, the place-sensitive policy form and the more place-based and led, bottom-up kind. In broad terms, the early regional policies were targeted on areas of greatest need, but were formulated and delivered in a centralized, top-down manner with limited opportunities for inputs or collaboration amongst local and regional actors. Much more progress on place-based and place-sensitive policy was achieved in Scotland and Wales through their dedicated (sub)national development agencies.[24] Incidences of more place-sensitive policies were evident too, for example, in relation to the geography of investment in then nationalized industries such as coal, shipbuilding and steel.[25]

Later regional policies were similarly largely centralized and top down with their focus on liberalizing factor markets and remedying market failures as the means to improving local and regional competitiveness.[26] Less emphasis was placed upon addressing the persistent structural problems negatively affecting such places in terms of weak demand, underdeveloped skills, lack of innovation and infrastructure deficits. The policies were more akin to spatially targeted, top-down approaches. However, devolution and constitutional change in the late 1990s enabled Northern Ireland, Scotland and Wales with new institutional arrangements, powers and resources to address their (sub)national economic and social development in more bottom-up, place-led ways.[27] Similarly, in England, the regional development agencies (RDAs) sought to address the underlying bases of regional productivity and were provided with some decentralization of powers and resources to enable local actors to better adapt policies to address local conditions and potentials.

Urban policies evolved from their earlier built environment focus to linking economic, social and infrastructural aims with a more pronounced market failure, economic development and geographical focus on the problems of especially inner-city areas.[28] Most schemes were spatially targeted, top-down spatial policy, especially in England. Innovations were particularly evident in area-based approaches in Scotland.[29] Such approaches evolved towards new institutional arrangements such as urban development corporations and more localized, neighbourhood-level initiatives and community participation in England.[30] Greater acknowledgement of the importance of place-sensitive policy and coordination developed over time, for example, in reversing overspill and urban population relocation policies and attempting to get national mainstream departments to recognize and prioritize their needs.

Despite sustained effort in recent decades, such policies have proved disappointing in terms of having any major or lasting impact on many of the depressed areas of the country. As the analysis in Chapters 1–4 demonstrate, the longstanding problems have persisted and cases of places able to turnaround their prospects are rare. At best, such policies may have only prevented geographical inequalities from worsening at a faster rate. It is vitally important in formulating policies as part of the "levelling up" agenda and addressing the plight of "left behind" places to learn from this long history of knowledge and experience. Below we distil the lessons from what has proven more effective at specific times and in particular places and identify the issues that have inhibited the positive contributions of policy.

Overall, in broad terms, there has been a somewhat mixed picture of implementing effective local, regional and urban policy in the UK. Much past spatial policy has been marked by more spatially targeted and spatially selective and insufficiently place-sensitive rather than more place-led, bottom-up, place-based approaches. There have been relatively limited moves towards more place-led, bottom-up forms of place-based policies in the devolved territories, during the RDAs episode in the 2000s and amongst some local enterprise partnerships (LEPs) and mayoral combined authorities in England since 2010. Indeed, since 2019, and specifically in England, there has been a shift back towards a more centralized, top-down, competitive bid-based and small-scale, spatially targeted approach, for example, with freeports, innovation zones and town deals.[31]

5.4 THE LIMITATIONS AND WEAKNESSES OF PAST POLICIES

It would be incorrect and misleading to suggest that past spatial policies have had no impact on "levelling up" the economic geography of the UK and addressing the problems of "left behind places". There is certainly evidence that regional policies helped to create significant numbers of jobs in the designated assisted areas during the 1960s, and to that extent they served at least to prevent the economic prospects and performance in those areas from being less favourable than would most likely have been otherwise.[32] And urban policies have undoubtedly helped to regenerate parts of the UK's major inner-city areas, including London. But the fact that over the past four decades or so spatial inequalities have widened significantly, as shown in Chapters 2 and 3, and weaker places have been ill-equipped to cope with and bounce back from economic shocks, as Chapter 4 demonstrates, suggests that past policies did not succeed in forging the economic transformation of the country's lagging cities, towns and localities on a scale sufficient to secure their long-term economic prospects, adaptability and competitiveness.

https://doi.org/10.1080/2578711X.2019.1547489

Table 5.4 Some key limitations and weaknesses of past spatial policy in the UK

- Lack of recognition of scale and importance of the "left behind" problem
- Insufficient resources committed to the problem
- Lack of a strategic vision for a spatially balanced economy
- Failure to take a holistic view of local economic development
- Failure to integrate regional policy with mainstream policymaking
- Overcentralized ("top down") approach to policy formulation and implementation
- Overemphasis on "one size fits all" policy measures
- Disruptive churn of policies and policy institutions
- Inadequate development of local policymaking capacity and capabilities

Source: Authors' own elaboration.

Critically, past policy in the UK has been bedevilled by several recurrent issues that have constrained progress and overall impact (Table 5.4). First, apart from the initiation of spatial policies to address their spatially uneven impacts in the recession-prone 1920s and 1930s, and the aftermath of the Second World War (1939–45), the UK government has never grasped or sufficiently prioritized the magnitude and importance of geographical inequalities as a national problem. Funding has, on the whole, been modest in relation to the scale of geographical inequalities across the UK and the size of the national economy. Priority and resource have not been of an ambition and scale necessary to address this longstanding and persistent issue.

In fact, obtaining estimates of expenditure on regional and other forms of spatial policy as these have evolve is, surprisingly, far from straightforward. Not even UK government departments appear to have such information.

We have estimated, for the first time to our knowledge, the policy public sector investment over the period 1960–2020.[33] A number of sources have been used to compile the estimates.[34] We estimate that, on average, HM Government has invested some £2.9 billion per annum in direct spatial policy (at 2020 real prices), equivalent to around 0.15% of gross national income (GNI) per annum over the 60-year period.[35] The European Union (EU), through Structural and Cohesion Policy support, has added around 0.125% per annum to this over the period since 1968. These expenditures are very small when expressed in these terms, certainly in relation to the scale and nature of the task which they are meant to address. They are also surprisingly small given that there is a strong body of evidence that suggests that the benefits from policy intervention can be substantial, reflecting a net rate of return to public sector investment of at least two-to-one.[36] Moreover, public sector investment of £1 has been associated with a leverage of private sector investment of up to three or even four.

The second key issue is the lack of a clear, focused, and sustained commitment and priority to reduce geographical inequalities. This failure has endured despite the pioneering history of the UK in recognizing the interrelationships between development in prosperous and poorer regions, and especially the dominance of London, in the Barlow Report.[37] Such inability to learn from its own policymaking history is, alas, not confined to the UK government.[38] But with respect to the UK, although under the New Labour government in the 2000s a cross-department target was established to reduce the gaps in growth rates between the UK regions, this did not take sufficient account of the different starting points and dynamics of each region (see Chapter 1). Moreover, the regional policy emphasis upon endogenous growth within regions in the 2000s meant powers and resources were decentralized to both richer and poorer regions through the RDAs in England, and in the particular institutional arrangements for economic development in the devolved territories (Northern Ireland, Scotland and Wales). This policy approach endowed already advantaged regions with institutional capacity and resources to support their further development, effectively treating "unequals equally" and failing to reduce overall geographical inequalities.[39]

The UK government's continued failure to coordinate and integrate policy between different areas and spatial levels is the third key issue. Since its inception 90 years ago, spatial policy in the UK has always been seen as a limited system of region- or city-specific aid quite separate from and unrelated to other forms of government policy and expenditure. "Non-spatial" government expenditures are vast compared with the sums devoted to "official" regional and urban policy. For example, mainstream UK total government expenditure in 2018/19 was some £855 billion.[40] Yet, almost every form of "non-spatial" expenditure programme has important direct and indirect—and crucially, differential—geographical impacts. Overall, some forms of identifiable public expenditure, which includes spatial policies, certainly favour lagging and less prosperous regions. But others are actually biased to the more prosperous regions.

Thus, within England, identifiable expenditure on employment measures tends to favour Northern and Midlands regions, as it should. But spending on economic development and enterprise, on science and technology, and on transport strongly favours London and the South East (Table 5.5). In this sense, they might thus be viewed as acting as "counter-regional policies", supporting and fostering growth in already-prosperous parts of the country rather than giving preference to areas that need to be "levelled up". Neglecting the spatial dimensions of national policy generates unforeseen geographical impacts and, in some cases, as mentioned above, can work counter to the objectives of spatial policies.

Another key problem has been the proliferation and churn of policy schemes and bodies.[42] The sheer proliferation of schemes and institutions is staggering, particularly over the past two decades, with diverse measures and interventions at a variety of spatial scales and fragmented coverage, with different foci and funding streams (Figure 5.1).

Further, many policy initiatives have had limited life spans, so there has also been a lack of continuity: churn does not make for strategic long-term planning. A broad shift has been evident over the past 40 years from fewer, longer term and better-resourced initiatives to multiple, shorter term and less well-resourced interventions.[44] The devolved administrations have experienced this problem too, with ongoing institutional and policy shifts in both Scotland and Wales.[45] A recurrent problem is that constant changes in institutions and policies have

https://doi.org/10.1080/2578711X.2019.1547489

Table 5.5 UK identifiable public expenditure by function per capita, 2017–18 to 2019–20 (indexed UK = 100)

	Economic affairs	...of which: enterprise and economic development	...of which: science and technology	...of which: employment policies	...of which: transport	Housing and community amenities
London	146	130	124	109	192	158
South East	103	127	120	57	90	66
East	91	75	104	63	95	68
South West	78	85	86	45	64	54
East Midlands	69	70	79	107	54	60
West Midlands	92	67	122	122	91	71
Yorkshire and Humberside	73	69	96	133	62	91
North West	85	82	76	122	94	63
North East	87	79	116	164	75	111
England	95	92	103	97	98	98
Scotland	139	149	96	118	138	210
Wales	98	116	72	101	83	141
Northern Ireland	110	144	41	126	69	213

Sources: Various UK government public spending by country and region.[41]

become the main responses to persistent geographical inequalities in a highly centralized system with powers concentrated at the national centre.

Closely related to centralization, limited, constrained and variable subnational funding and financing for local, regional and urban policy is the fifth key issue. This problem has persisted due to the continued national government dominance and centralized design and control of levels, duration and terms of funding, as well as the autonomies and flexibilities in its utilization.[46] While it is less pronounced beyond England in the devolved territories, even here the local, regional and urban actors perceive centralized control at the (sub)national government level.[47] Meaningful decentralization of powers and resources is critical to enable actors to formulate appropriate policy mixes to address their particular circumstances and potentials. Local governments key role is to play as democratically elected and accountable local institutions with multiple functions and responsibilities. Their role is currently hampered by the uneven legacies of a decade of austerity and uncertain future funding arrangements and levels.[48] The last critical issue is the uneven, under-developed and weak subnational strategic research, intelligence, monitoring and evaluation capacity. The long history of centralized governance in the UK and relatively limited decentralization of powers and resources have

Figure 5.1 Proliferation and churn of spatial policy schemes and bodies in the UK, 1978–2018

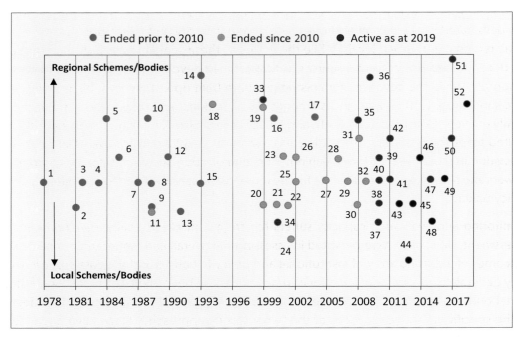

1. Urban Programme (expansion)
2. Urban Development Corporations
3. Urban Development Grant
4. Derelict Land Grant
5. Regional Development Grant (revision)
6. City Action Teams
7. Urban Regeneration Grant
8. City Grant
9. Inner City Compacts
10. Regional Enterprise Grant
11. Action for Cities
12. Training and Enterprise Council
13. City Challenge
14. English Partnerships
15. Single Regeneration Budget
16. Enterprise Grant Scheme
17. Selective Finance for Investment
18. Government Offices for the Regions
19. Regional Development Agencies
20. New Deal for Communities
21. Urban Regeneration Companies
22. Neighbourhood Renewal Fund
23. Local Strategic Partnerships
24. Neighbourhood Management Pathfinders
25. Local Authority Business Growth Incentive
26. Housing Market Renewal Pathfinders

27. Working Neighbourhoods Fund
28. Local Area Agreements
29. Local Enterprise Growth Initiative
30. City/Economic Development Companies
31. Multi-Area Agreements/City Region Pilots
32. Future Jobs Fund
33. National Coalfields Programme
34. Business Improvement Districts
35. Grants for Business Investment
36. Homes and Communities Agency
37. Community Budgets
38. Enterprise Zones (new phase)
39. Regional Growth Fund
40. Local Enterprise Partnerships
41. Growing Places Fund
42. Combined Authorities
43. City Deals
44. Business Rate Retention
45. Tax Increment Finance
46. Devolution Deals
47. Local Growth Fund
48. Coastal Communities Fund
49. Mayoral Development Corporations
50. Combined authority Mayors
51. Industrial Strategy White Paper
52. UK Shared Prosperity Fund

Source: Adapted from the National Audit Office (NAO).[43]

undermined the ability of local, regional and urban actors to develop their strategic policy-making and delivery capacity. Actors have been trapped in a bind where national government has dominated policymaking and perceives limited capacity and innovation to exist at the local, regional and urban levels, while the actors at these spatial scales lack the appropriate decentralized powers and resources to support their development of strategic ideas and proposals. While the devolved administrations have built upon their long history and policymaking capacity, the experiences amongst local, regional and urban actors in England is highly uneven.[49] The historical weight and legacy of centralized, top-down policymaking has limited scope for local capacity building and discretion, despite moves towards some decentralization in recent years. More meaningful decentralization and devolution of appropriate powers and resources is a prerequisite for the more "place-sensitive" and "place-based" spatial policymaking.

Monitoring and evaluation capacity suffers too from centralized policy management and assessment. Difficulties have persisted in assessing the overall and longer term impacts and outcomes of a shifting array of institutional and policy initiatives and the data requirements they generate. Successes and areas for improvement have been identified in the long history of national evaluations.[50] Such concerns have been recognized and addressed to a degree in the specifically economic focus of the "what works" approach.[51] Steps have been made towards improving the use of evidence and robust monitoring and evaluation frameworks to inform local, regional and urban policymaking.[52] But such moves need further resource support to deepen and accelerate their advance. While drawn from the analysis of our critical case of the UK, many of these five key issues are relevant and resonant in other national settings.

5.5 CONCLUSIONS: LESSONS FROM THE PAST

This chapter has sought to provide a better understanding of what is meant by spatial policy intervention. It has distinguished three distinct types of spatial intervention; spatially targeted, place sensitive and "place based".

The evidence is that much of British spatial policy has been spatially targeted and spatially selective, but far more limited when it comes to being place led and bottom up. Clearly, a better understanding of the relative advantages and disadvantages of these different types of spatial intervention is required in order to devise appropriate and successful "place-based policies" to address the economic problems faced by "left behind places", but a key message from the analysis is that past UK policies have been underfunded, inconsistent, and been inadequately tailored and adapted to the needs of different local economies.

Our rather crude estimates suggest that discretionary expenditure in the UK on urban and regional policy when both domestic and EU spatial policy were in operation was equivalent to only 0.27% of the UK annual GNI (2020 prices). This is a relatively modest amount in the light of the scale of the economic challenges being addressed. A decisive and effective "levelling up" programme will require far more resources.

If the needs of "left behind places" are to be addressed more effectively by building on a place-led and more bottom-up approach, there has to be more decentralization of power and resources to place-based agencies. Moreover, and crucially for relative success, place-based efforts have to be coordinated and aligned with place-sensitive national policies. We argue that the key challenge of a UK levelling up mission is to integrate place-based policies with greater place sensitivity in national policies and in regulation and mainstream spending. This will require the reform of priorities and institutions at a national scale. In the past the two have been poorly coordinated and have rarely been aligned, indeed the former have frequently been swamped and undermined by the latter. Resolving this misalignment is critical to securing effective outcomes.

NOTES

[1] Parsons DW (1986) *The Political Economy of British Regional Policy*. London: Croom Helm.

[2] Garcilazo JE, Martins JO and Tompson W (2010) Why policies may need to be place-based in order to be people-centred. *VoxEU.org*, 20 November; Gill I (2010) Regional development policies: Place-based or people-centred? *VoxEU.org*, 9 October.

[3] Beer A, McKenzie F, Blažek J, Sotarauta M and Ayres S (2020) *Every Place Matters: Towards Effective Place-Based Policy* (RSA Policy Impact Book Series). London: Routledge.

[4] Cheshire P, Nathan M and Overman H (2014) *Urban Economics and Policy*. Aldershot: Edward Elgar; World Bank (2009) *Reshaping Economic Geography*. Washington, DC: World Bank.

[5] Bolton R (1992) "Place prosperity vs people prosperity" revisited: An old issue with a new angle. *Urban Studies*, 29: 185–203.

[6] Barca F (2009) *An Agenda for a Reformed Cohesion Policy* (Independent report prepared at the request of Danuta Hubner, Commissioner for Regional Policy); Barca F, McCann P and Rodríguez-Pose A (2012) The case for regional development intervention: Place-based versus place-neutral approaches. *Journal of Regional Science*, 52: 134–152.

[7] Neumark D and Simpson H (2014) *Place-Based Policies* (Working Paper No. 20049). Cambridge, MA: National Bureau of Economic Research (NBER).

[8] Austin B, Glaeser E and Summers L (2018) *Jobs for the Heartland: Place-Based Policies in 21st Century America*. Washington DC: Brookings Institution.

[9] Overman H (2020) *People, Places and Politics: Policy Challenges* (CEP 2019 Election Analysis Series). London: London School of Economics (LSE).

[10] Neumark D and Simpson H (2014) *Place-Based Policies* (Working Paper No. 20049). Cambridge, MA:

https://doi.org/10.1080/2578711X.2019.1547489

National Bureau of Economic Research (NBER).

[11] Iammarino S, Rodríguez-Pose A and Storper M (2018) Regional inequality in Europe: Evidence, theory and policy implications. *Journal of Economic Geography*, 19: 273–298.

[12] Barca (2009), see Reference 6.

[13] Barca et al. (2012), at 139, see Reference 6.

[14] Bailey D, Pitelis C and Tomlinson PR (2018) A place-based developmental regional industrial strategy for sustainable capture of co-created value. *Cambridge Journal of Economics*, 42: 1521–1542.

[15] Alessandrini M , Celotti, P, Dallhammer, E, Gorny, H, Gramillano, A, Schuh, B, Zingaretti, C, Toptsidou, M, and Gaupp-Berghausen, M (2019) *Implementing a Place-Based Approach to EU Industrial Policy Strategy*. Brussels: European Committee of the Regions, Commission for Economic Policy.

[16] Beer et al. (2020), see Reference 3.

[17] Beer et al. (2020), see Reference 3.

[18] Morgan K (2020) The future of place-based innovation policy (as if "lagging regions" really mattered). In M Barzotto, C Corradini, F Fai, S Labory and P Tomlinson (eds.), *Revitalising Lagging Regions: Smart Specialisation and Industry 4.0*, pp. 79–90. London: Routledge.

[19] Parsons (1986), see Reference 1.

[20] Barlow, M (1940) *Report of Royal Commission on the Distribution of the Industrial Population*. London: HMSO.

[21] McCrone G (1969) *Regional Policy in Britain*. London: George Allen & Unwin; Parsons (1986), see Reference 1.

[22] Such as under the Margaret Thatcher governments in the 1980s. As regional inequalities widened in that decade, and the "North–South divide" debate erupted accordingly, Lord Young, the then Secretary of State for Trade and Industry, and the member of the Cabinet responsible for regional policy, actually rejected the need for such intervention with a simple and unapologetic appeal to the "justice of history": "There was more industrialisation in the North, originally, therefore there now has to be more deindustrialisation. Until 70 years ago the North was always the richest part of the country. […] Now some of it is in the South. It's our turn, that's all" (quoted in UK Parliament, 1987, *Hansard Business*, vol 489, at 48). Table 2.1 in Chapter 2 suggests that this line of reasoning was in fact quite erroneous.

[23] Martin RL (1988) The political economy of Britain's North–South divide. *Transactions of the Institute of British Geographers*, 13: 389–418; Martin RL (1993a) Remapping British regional policy: The end of the North–South divide? *Regional Studies*, 27: 797–805; Martin RL (1993b) Reviving the economic case for regional policy. In RT Harrison and P Townroe (eds.), *Spatial Policy in a Divided Nation*, pp. 270–290. London: Jessica Kingsley; Moore BC, Rhodes J and Tyler P (1986). *The Effects of Government Regional Policy*. London: HMSO, 1986; Rhodes J, Tyler P and Brennan A (2007) *The Single Regeneration Budget— Final Evaluation*. Cambridge: Department of Land Economy, University of Cambridge. https://www.landecon.cam.ac.uk/system/files/documents/SRB_part1_finaleval_feb07.pdf/; Taylor J and Wren C (1997) UK regional policy: An evaluation. *Regional Studies*, 31: 835–848.

[24] Bellini N, Danson M and Halkier H (2012) *Regional Development Agencies: The Next Generation?* New

York: Routledge.

[25] Hudson R (1989) *Wrecking a Region: State Policies, Party Politics and Regional Change in North East England*. London: Pion.

[26] Martin (1993a, 1993b), see Reference 23.

[27] Bellini et al. (2012), see Reference 24.

[28] Oatley N (ed.) (1998) *Cities, Economic Competition and Urban Policy*. Thousand Oaks, CA: Sage.

[29] Pacione M (2009) *Urban Geography: A Global Perspective*. London: Routledge.

[30] Oatley (1998), see Reference 28.

[31] Pike A, Kempton L, MacKinnon D, O'Brien P and Tomaney J (2020) *Evidence for the Devolution All-Party Parliamentary Group*. Newcastle upon Tyne: CURDS, Newcastle University. https://www.ncl.ac.uk/media/wwwnclacuk/curds/files/CURDS%20evidence%20for%20the%20Devolution%20APPG%20inquiry.pdf/.

[32] A key difficulty in assessing the impact of past policies is that of specifying a realistic and meaningful "counterfactual" position, that is, an estimate of what would have happened in the assisted areas in the absence of regional aid.

[33] Estimating expenditure on urban and regional policy is not at all easy. To the authors' knowledge there has been no systematic attempt to record expenditure systematically. The tendency for the type of policy initiatives to change with successive governments and, importantly, the way they have been delivered has complicated matters considerably. In more recent years, and particularly since the time in England of the RDAs, it has been very difficult to separate out urban and regional policy expenditure, and the recent moves to providing funds on the basis of growth deal funding has complicated matters even further. Two important sources in relation to UK regional policy are: Moore et al. (1986), see Reference 23; Wren C (2005) Regional grants: Are they worth it? *Fiscal Studies*, 26, 245–275; and Taylor and Wren (1997), see Reference 23. Our estimate of expenditure on regional policy over the period 1961–92 is £63.1 billion constant 2020 prices. The only source we have to compare this estimate with is that of Wren (2005), who derived an estimate of £53.76 billion constant 2020 prices. Our combined estimate of expenditure on both urban and regional policy in the UK over the entire period 1961–2020 is of the order of £174.5 billion constant 2020 prices. This would translate into an estimate of 0.15% per annum constant 2020 prices averaged over 60 years. The main source of evidence on expenditure relating to EU Structural Fund and Cohesion Policy is the work of Bachtler, J and Begg, I (2017) Cohesion policy after Brexit: the economic, social and institutional challenges, *Journal of Social Policy*, 46(4), 745–763. They suggest that EU regional policy may have contributed £66 billion (nominal) of funding over broadly the period since the late 1970s through to 2020, roughly equivalent to 0.1% of the UK's GNI (nominal). Although there is clearly much uncertainty, we have adopted a range of £57–66 billion and translated this into constant 2020 prices. A key problem is that we do not have estimates of how the funding was apportioned over the early part of the period 1975–late 1980s. On the basis of the data, we have we would suggest that the EU funding was in a range of 0.12–0.16%, but it is probably best to prefer the lower estimate until more data can be obtained. Overall, our rather crude estimates suggest that discretionary expenditure in the UK on urban and regional policy when both domestic and EU policy were available has been over the last 60 years has been equivalent to some 0.27% of the UK's GNI (2020 prices). European regional policy support has often been deployed on the basis of a model of matched co-financing from domestic UK

spatial policy funds, broadly on the basis of 50%, although the precise co-financing percentage has varied considerably by programme and over time. It should also be remembered that UK regional and urban policy has also usually required the projects and partners supported to provide funding and the ability of urban policy expenditure to lever other funds into the regeneration process has been an important feature. The amount of extra funding leveraged has varied considerably, but it has not been uncommon for leverage to be of the order of three-to-one, particularly when it comes to property related regeneration.

[34] Moore et al. (1986) see Reference 23; Taylor and Wren (1997), see Reference 23; Wren (2005), see Reference 33.

[35] This compares with around 0.7% of GNI (£14 billion in 2019) the UK government has spent on international aid in recent years (see https://www.gov.uk/government/statistics/statistics-on-international-development-final-uk-aid-spend-2019/statistics-on-international-development-final-uk-aid-spend-2019). Mainstream UK total government expenditure in 2018–19 was some £855 billion in real terms (HM Treasury, 2019). See reference 40.

[36] Tyler P, Warnock C, Provins A and Lanz B (2011) Valuing the benefits of urban regeneration. *Urban Studies*, 50: 169–190.

[37] Barlow (1940), see Reference 20.

[38] Haddon C, Devanny J, Forsdick C and Thompson A (2015) *What is the Value of History in Policymaking?* London: Institute of Government.

[39] Morgan K (2006) Devolution and development: Territorial justice and the North–South divide. *Publius*, 36: 189–206.

[40] HM Treasury (2019) *Public Expenditure Statistical Analysis 2019*. London: HM Treasury.

[41] For example, see https://www.gov.uk/government/statistics/country-and-regional-analysis-2020/.

[42] Martin RL, Bailey D, Evenhuis E, Gardener B, Pike A, Sunley P and Tyler P (2019) *The Economic Performance of Britain's Cities: Patterns, Processes and Policy Implications* (Economic and Social Research Council (ESRC) Structural Transformation, Adaptability and City Economic Evolutions Research Project). www.cityevolutions.org.uk/.

[43] National Audit Office (NAO) (2019) *Local Enterprise Partnerships: An Update on Progress*. London: NAO.

[44] National Audit Office (NAO) (2013) *Funding and Structures for Local Economic Growth*. London: NAO; NAO (2019), see Reference 43; Pacione M (2009) *Urban Geography: A Global Perspective*. London: Routledge.

[45] Clelland D (2020) Beyond the city region? Uneven governance and the evolution of regional economic development in Scotland. *Local Economy*, 35: 7–26.

[46] NAO (2013), see Reference 44.

[47] Clelland (2020), see Reference 45; Organisation for Economic Co-operation and Development (OECD) (2020) *The Future of Regional Development and Public Investment in Wales, United Kingdom*. Paris: OECD.

[48] Gray M and Barford A (2018) The depths of the cuts: The uneven geography of local government austerity. *Cambridge Journal of Regions, Economy and Society*, 11: 541–563.

[49] Harding A and Holden J (2015) *Using Evidence: Greater Manchester Case Study*. London: What Works Centre for Local Economic Growth.

[50] Moore et al. (1986), see Reference 23.

[51] What Works Network (2014) *What Works: Evidence for Decision-Makers*. London: What Works Network.

[52] Harding and Holden (2015), see Reference 49.

6. INSTITUTIONS AND POLICIES FOR "LEVELLING UP" AND "LEFT BEHIND PLACES"

Keywords: rethinking the 'national' economy, mission-oriented levelling up policy, devolution, multi-level federal polity, new financial models

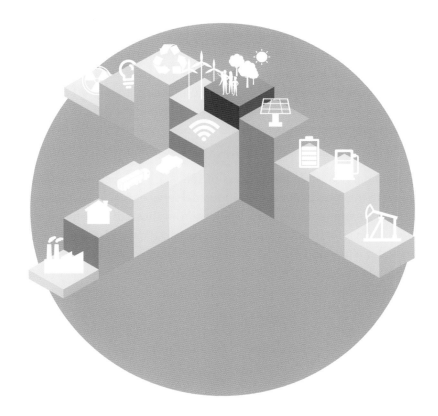

The geographic divide between thriving and broken cities is not inevitable … But it cannot be reversed by small adjustments to public policies. Trivially, small is insufficient, but more fundamentally, spatial dynamics depend on expectations … Expectations are currently anchored on the changes of recent decades, and so momentum is self-fulfilling. To change this requires a policy change sufficiently large to shock expectations into a different configuration.[1]

6.1. KEY FINDINGS AND THEIR POLICY IMPLICATIONS

The preceding chapters have set out the scale of the economic problem of "left behind places" in the UK, and reviewed previous policy approaches pursued over many decades to "level up" or "rebalance" the country's economic geography. Our findings reveal just how complex is the challenge of "levelling up" Britain's "left behind places". The key issue is that the problem of spatial economic inequality across the country is not some recent feature or aberration, but has been long in the making, associated with cumulative processes of regional and local divergence since the early 1980s, with antecedents going back much earlier than that, even to the inter-war years, or further still.

There is little evidence that cost advantages in Northern areas are correcting and offsetting cumulative processes in the spatial development of skilled labour and human capital and the quality of the residential and business environment. While output, employment, wage and productivity patterns show important geographical variations across the country, it is clear that a series of local authority districts suffer from multiple types of under-performance on several or all of these metrics. The performance of these "left behind places" has progressively fallen away from the national average, and while the pace of this divergent development has varied over time, the overall trend has been remarkably persistent over the period. The "left behind problem" has become spatially and systemically entrenched.

The primary cause of this process of spatial divergence lies in the inability of some places to adapt to the growth of the post-industrial service and knowledge-based economy whose locational requirements are very different from those of past heavy industries. These processes have been reinforced by cumulative spatially differentiated interactions between skills supply and labour demand. Further, some government economic policies from the early 1980s, favouring market forces and financial and related activities, have reinforced the spatial imbalance of the economy. While the effects of the major shocks and recessions that have disrupted the economy over the past 40 years or so have in some ways become more varied and harder to predict, and the economic resilience of localities differs significantly, the uneven geography of recoverability shows a degree of continuity over successive recessions. The consequences of

https://doi.org/10.1080/2578711X.2021.1992172

the Covid-19 pandemic have been most severe in many of the local authority areas with poor economic performance and high levels of social deprivation. On the basis of our analysis of past resilience, the patterns of recovery from the current recession are highly likely to repeat this pattern and significantly worsen spatial inequalities.

The evidence presented in Chapter 5 indicated that past policies in the UK have reflected a lack of recognition of the scale and importance of the "left-behind" problem and that insufficient resources have been committed to it. Moreover, the objective of achieving a more spatially balanced economy has not been incorporated into *mainstream* policymaking. The traditional approach, particularly when compared with other countries, has reflected an over-centralized ("top-down") system of policy formulation and implementation, often leading to an overemphasis on the application of "one size fits all" policy measures. The political cycle has then often led to a disruptive churn of policies and policy institutions. Moreover, and seemingly at odds with development in other countries, particularly in Europe, there has been inadequate development of local policymaking capacity and capabilities, including the ability to monitor and track the nature of the problem and the impact of policy on it.

The conclusion from all this can be simply stated: the scale and nature of the UK's contemporary "left behind places" problem are such that only a transformative shift in policy model and resource commitment of historic proportions are likely to achieve the "levelling up" ambition that has become such a prominent theme in the current government's political declarations. The immensity and difficulty of the "levelling up" policy challenge cannot be exaggerated. As Paul Collier intimates above, the problem of "left behind places" in the UK, and other Western societies is deeply rooted: it is a self-fulfilling and self-reinforcing outcome of the economic, political, and institutional configurations and priorities that have held sway over the past four decades or more. Changing those configurations and priorities is now imperative not only to achieve more socially and spatially equitable economic outcomes, a new "economics of belonging" as Sandbu would put it,[2] but also to ensure that the transition to a green, net zero carbon future is socially and spatially just.

Given this imperative, the aim in this chapter is not to set down a long list of particular policy instruments, of this and that specific measure, that could help to achieve "levelling up", but rather to suggest some fundamental principles and precepts on which a meaningful and successful "levelling up" strategy will need to be based. While focusing on the UK's predicament and experience, the discussion also seeks to identify issues of broader relevance for localities, cities and regions that might be applicable in other national settings. The main arguments are about taking place seriously, and thinking about the local, regional and urban routes by which a clear and binding national mission of "levelling up" can reduce spatial inequalities.

6.2 GRASPING THE TRANSFORMATIVE MOMENT FOR LOCAL, REGIONAL AND URBAN DEVELOPMENT POLICY

Localities, regions and cities across the world face unprecedented and uncertain situations in the wake of the momentous disruptions of the last decade, including the global financial crisis and the Covid-19 pandemic, and the upheavals that will unfold in the coming decades due to climate change, and the march of artificial intelligence (AI).[3] Specific national settings face their own combinations of such problems. The UK is also having to confront the particular and uncertain impacts of Brexit on its trading relationships with the European Union (EU) and the rest of the world.[4] These several events and developments pose key challenges for regional, urban and local economies, but also, at the same time, an historic opportunity for states to embark on policy programmes that will actually achieve the "rebalancing" and "levelling up" that have become part of today's political lexicon. It is an opportunity that must not be wasted. Not taking this opportunity will almost certainly see spatial inequalities widen yet further.

State responses to both the global financial crisis and the Covid-19 pandemic have departed from the neoliberal and market-based political-economic model of recent decades: these historic shocks have shown how "the state is back" and can intervene on a massive scale if circumstances require.[5] The scale of state and central bank support for the banking system in the global financial crisis was unprecedented in the post-war era. It was unfortunate, however, that public services at the national and local levels were made to pay for that state support to the banks by the imposition of several years of "fiscal consolidation", that is, austerity. We now know that the brunt of the cuts to social and other public services fell particularly on "left behind places", adding to their predicament.[6]

Across the global system, the collapse of economic output due to the Covid-19 pandemic was of historic proportions—in some countries, the UK included, the fall was the worst on record, far deeper than in the great recession following the global financial crisis.[7] As governments across the globe imposed restrictions and "lockdowns" in the public health crisis, they also expended huge sums of money to support workers, jobs and businesses, amounting to more than three times the monies spent during the financial crisis.[8] It is estimated that globally more than US$12 trillion has been committed. Some US$4 trillion of this has been in Western Europe alone, amounting to more than 20 times today's value of the Marshall Plan for post-Second World War reconstruction (Box 6.1).

This dramatic increase in state intervention and fiscal stimulus in response to the pandemic across the world has stimulated calls for yet further large-scale involvement to support economic, social and environmental recovery, to "build back better", and to reconstruct national economies in fairer, more inclusive and greener ways for the post-pandemic era.[10] Both the UK's *Build Back Better: Our Plan for Growth* (2021) and the United States' *Build Back Better Agenda* (2021) embody this commitment, though they differ somewhat in focus, and considerably in

 https://doi.org/10.1080/2578711X.2021.1992172

Box 6.1 The "European Recovery Programme" (Marshall Plan), 1948

The European Recovery Programme was a US-led initiative that aimed to provide aid to support the recovery of Western European countries after the conflict of the Second World War. The plan sought to finance urban, industrial and infrastructure reconstruction, and to promote economic integration and trade within Europe and with the United States. Amidst the geoeconomics and geopolitical setting of the post-war period, it aimed to ensure the rebuilding of liberal, democratic and mixed economies in the major countries of France, Germany and the UK. The programme was worth US\$15 billion at the time—around US\$167 billion in today's money. It was known as the Marshall Plan after its champion, the then US Secretary of State, George Marshall.

Source: Agnew and Entrikin.[9]

---

the scale of resources that are likely to be devoted to the task. Other similar calls have been made for Green New Deals.[11]

If carried through, the intended scale of the present US Build Back Better programme is estimated at around US\$6 trillion or more over the next eight years.[12] This expenditure would be the biggest fiscal stimulus to the US economy since the New Deal of 1930. The ambition and size of the programme has been shaped by the experience of what has been interpreted as the inadequate and insufficiently bold response to the global financial crisis and its perceived impact in hindering a more robust and faster recovery. Like the New Deal, the Build Back Better plan will include public works, investment support for industry, new institutional building, welfare programmes and regulatory reforms.

In the UK under the Build Back Better plan, some £30 billion has been allocated, of which £4.8 billion is referred to as the "Levelling Up Fund". This total of £30 billion, to be spread over the next five years or so, would be equivalent to approximately 0.25% per annum of 2020 gross national income (GNI). This is to be compared with £14.5 billion spent in 2020 on international aid (0.7% of GNI). As the evidence in Chapter 5 showed, historically UK urban and regional policy and resources provided by the EU through Structural Funds and Cohesion Policy *taken together* have amounted to about 0.25% of UK GNI per annum. It is not clear yet whether the proposed Shared Prosperity Fund will provide the same level of resource, but even if it does, the "New Deal for Left Behind Places" in the UK looks very modest indeed compared with its American counterpart and the sheer scale of the problem being addressed. An annual commitment to, say, £20 billion (in real terms) *per annum* would still only amount to approximately 1% of 2020 GNI.

By way of another comparison, Germany has spent €2 trillion since 1990 on its *Aufbau Ost* programme to level up per capita incomes in the former East Germany to those in the West. This equates to around €70 billion per annum, or approximately £55 billion. Interestingly, this is roughly what Lord Heseltine in his 2012 report *No Stone Unturned* argued was the annual sum of central Government spending that could be devolved to local bodies across England.

As Chapter 5 explains, the historical experience of previous economic transitions and their management by the state in the UK have generated profoundly uneven geographical effects and legacies. Deindustrialization and the shift to a service-dominated economy continue to mark the predicaments and potentials of the "left behind places" across the UK, as Chapters 1–4 demonstrate. Certain areas, such as the coalfield communities that lost their mining industry in the 1980s, have taken a generation to recover levels of employment, and these areas are now reconfigured with very different social, gender, sectoral and job characteristics, often with a distinct shortage of "good" job opportunities.[13]

The current circumstances of unprecedented change and immense state involvement and ambition in recovery facing the UK and other countries across the world present something of a watershed moment in transforming local, regional and urban development policy. The move to a net zero carbon economy provides great opportunities to ensure that the geography of adaptation works to the advantage of "left behind places", many of which led the former carbon-based industrial economy. The need for a radical step change is clear and pressing. Relying on existing approaches risks reproducing the problems of merely ameliorating rather than resolving spatial inequalities, and addressing their symptoms rather than underlying causes. Given the levels of social and political discontent seen since the 2008 crisis and, in some cases, their reinforcement due to specific governments' handling of the Covid-19 pandemic,[14] this juncture presents an opportunity that politicians and policymakers would be wise not to waste. Critically, the UK state should grasp the current moment to craft transformative policy at a suitably momentous scale and learn from the under-powered response to the 2008 crash and its weak, uneven recovery.

6.3 ESTABLISHING A CLEAR AND BINDING NATIONAL MISSION FOR "LEVELLING UP"

While "levelling up" has been promoted as a defining agenda by the current UK government, such politically useful phrases require translation into strategic policy with clearer vision, definitions and targets. The lack of specific content, policies and novelty in the UK government's agenda has attracted criticism.[15] The UK government has articulated a collection of broad areas and policies including town regeneration, city growth, infrastructure, freeports, and innovation and research and development (R&D) in its national *Building Back Better: Our Plan for Growth*.[16] A Levelling Up Unit has now been established within the Cabinet Office, and a Levelling Up White Paper is promised, which will set out what the UK government means by "levelling up", and what policies it intends to follow to achieve that goal.

Regional Studies Policy Impact Books

https://doi.org/10.1080/2578711X.2021.1992172

Rather than just another specific civil service group and yet one more policy fund, our argument is that the scale of the "left behind" problem demands that addressing spatial inequalities becomes a central national priority with a clear and more (preferably legally) binding commitment, key published milestones and commensurate resources. Establishing a special group within the Cabinet Office is reminiscent of the New Labour government's Social Exclusion Unit in 1997. Whatever the merits of this approach, it is important that lessons should be learned about how to ensure that any new unit has a fixity in the institutional landscape and thus likely to have a real and lasting impact. Repeating the history of spatial policy summarized in Chapter 5 will lead to further muddled and inconsistent aims with piecemeal and under-resourced policies that risk failing to match the magnitude and scale of the challenges and opportunities of the current moment.

While the 2008 crash was followed by various ambitions for a "Green New Deal" in the UK and elsewhere,[17] the following decade revealed highly geographically uneven resilience and recovery and often disappointing results in reconstructing local, regional and urban economies.[18] Learning from past policy history (Chapter 5), and given the magnitude of the events from 2020, strategy must seek to avoid repeating the mistakes of recent decades.

In short, a mission-oriented approach is required. One of the crucial prerequisites for setting out a mission-oriented "levelling up" programme is a political rethink of both the meaning of "the economy" and of "spatial economic policy". Although some mainstream economists have at last recognized and appreciated that "the economy" does not reside on the head of the proverbial pin, the fact is that the key organs of policymaking in the UK, especially HM Treasury and the Bank of England, do not take the country's regional and urban structure into account in their models of the economy, the very models that underpin much of macro-economic policymaking.[19] A major corrective to this "nation as economy" model is required. It is in individual cities, towns and localities that the "everyday business of economic life" is conducted: where production is carried out, exports originate, wages are earned and partly spent, and social and public services are provided and accessed. The spatial structure and organization of the economy is not some incidental feature but foundational to how well the national economy performs, functions and prospers: geography matters. A new "spatial imaginary" needs to become an integral feature of political economic thinking and national economic management.

This would imply, secondly, that spatial (regional, urban and local) policy be treated not as separate from, but as integral to, national policymaking and objectives. Spatial policy has always been viewed as an adjunct to national economic policy. Moreover, the case for spatial policies has been repeatedly beset by two arguments—propagated by economists and frequently adopted by policymakers alike—that need to be put to rest. The first is that the only justification for spatial policies is on the grounds of correcting "market failures". Whilst policy should clearly be targeted to remove the impediments in land, labour and capital markets that are preventing adjustment in "left-behind" economies, it is important that this rationale for policy intervention does not translate into the belief that if only "market forces" were allowed to operate "freely" then there would be no significant problem of spatial economic inequality. In fact, there is now both strong theoretical arguments and empirical evidence to indicate that if indeed left unfettered, market forces tend to lead to the increasing concentration of economic activity in certain places rather than others, that is, to increasing spatial economic inequality.

Second, a recurring claim has been that there is an unavoidable tension between seeking greater spatial equality of economic outcomes ("levelling up"), on the one hand, and faster national economic growth, on the other: a negative "trade-off" between equality and efficiency. In the UK, this pernicious "trade-off" thesis has often been invoked, implicitly if not explicitly, to argue that policies aimed at boosting growth in lagging and "left behind places" must not in any way limit growth in London, the "dynamo" of the national economy. British Prime Minister Boris Johnson, when Mayor of London, exemplified this belief in his speech to the 2009 Conservative Party Conference when he informed civic leaders of Manchester, Leeds and Newcastle that "if you want to stimulate [your cities] then you invest in London, because London is the motor not just of the south-east, not just of England, not just of Britain, but of the whole of the UK economy".[20] London, he argued, was where the government would get the "biggest bang for its buck". A dynamic London is undoubtedly of benefit to the whole economy, but equally, thriving cities, towns and localities are also of benefit both to London and to the national economy as a whole. There is in fact little persuasive evidence of a trade-off between equality and efficiency; on the contrary, the evidence suggests that those countries with lower levels of social and spatial inequality tend to grow just as fast, if not faster, over the long run than those with greater disparities.[21]

Our argument, then, is that the UK government should articulate "levelling up" as a clear, explicit and binding national mission, akin to its net zero carbon commitment, and with a legally binding underpinning. This move would shift "levelling up" from a political slogan to a core mission to focus UK recovery efforts and enable government to be held to account. It also reflects the rise of mission-oriented forms of innovation and policy internationally to tackle complex, difficult and longstanding challenges such as climate change and demographic shifts (Table 6.1 and Box 6.2).[23] As Mazzucato and Dibb recognize,[24] addressing complex economic and social problems is profoundly more difficult than technological challenges, as the former are "wicked" challenges that require a mix of economic, political, regulatory and behavioural changes. Nevertheless, the importance of building a strong common public purpose around which public, private and civic actors can collaborate and construct innovative projects is key to progress in resolving many societal challenges.

The national "levelling up" mission could then be articulated as a clear and explicit commitment with wide support, for example, closing the gaps between specified geographies in a

https://doi.org/10.1080/2578711X.2021.1992172

Table 6.1 Some key pillars of a mission-oriented "levelling up" strategy

Re-envisioning the economy	Moving beyond a "nation as economy model" to one in which every region, city and town is recognized as integral and essential to national prosperity
Setting clear legally binding "levelling up" targets	Specification of maximum acceptable spatial differences in key local economic indicators (such as employment rate, productivity, gross domestic product (GDP) per capita), and per capita equality in critical public services provision (such as education, transport and health)
Embedding geography into national policymaking	Evaluating regional and subregional impact of mainstream macroeconomic policymaking, and ensuring those policies take explicit account of differing regional and local needs and priorities
Establishing nationwide devolved system of local economic development and governance	A federated territorial system of accountable city-region bodies/authorities charged with delivering and monitoring holistic socio-economic development strategies
Binding commitment of financial resources appropriate to the task	Legally binding central funding agreement as a fixed percentage of annual gross national income (GNI), for local economic, social, infrastructural and environment schemes. Plus new system of local authority economic development ("leveling up") bonds; and a regionalized business bank

range of key indicators relative to appropriate benchmarks over a set time period. Given the differences in national and subnational conditions and contexts, what those gaps, geographies, indicators, benchmarks and time periods are is a matter for deliberation and agreement rather than a fixed and predetermined formula. As Chapter 1 explains, understanding the upsides, downsides, and balances and priorities between various indicators is important, too. In the UK case, economic indicators that include productivity, earnings, unemployment and employment rates have been proposed.[25] Others have sought a wider range of economic measures alongside social and environmental indicators, including educational qualifications achievement and life expectancy, and a community needs index with an emphasis upon civic infrastructure.[26]

Box 6.2   Mission-oriented innovation and policy

Tackling the complex, challenging and large-scale economic, social and environmental issues—or grand challenges—faced by humanity requires innovative approaches. Making progress towards achieving such challenges requires breaking down efforts into pragmatic steps that can be taken through collaboration between public, private and civic actors. These are termed "missions": "concrete targets within a challenge that act as frames and stimuli for innovation". Such missions then set the direction for public policy efforts and investment towards solutions, but crucially they do not specify in detail how success can be achieved and any "right" answers are not known in advance. Missions stimulate the development of a range of different potential solutions and incentivise relevant actors to experiment and take risks.

Source: Mazzucato and Dibb.[22]

The scale of resources to support this national mission would need to be commensurate with the task. As noted above, the magnitude needs to be more aligned to that of a Marshall Plan than more modest, shorter term and fragmented individual funding initiatives. Learning from current international approaches,[27] funding could come from a combination of sources including tax reforms and increases, municipal bonds, long-term borrowing, and sovereign guarantees.

The national mission would need to be broken down into clearly specified aims and targets against which progress could be monitored and assessed and the government held to account. Having such a clear, longer term and strategic goal would serve to impart greater degree of continuity as well as adaptability to guard against the UK's endemic problems of shifting aims and institutional and policy churn and fragmentation.

Establishing such a clear and binding national mission in this way is challenging. Indeed, concerns are evident in the UK that "levelling up" risks remaining a popular slogan and being dominated by shorter term political calculation of electoral advantage.[28] An emergent "Southern discontent" is evident, too, as relatively more prosperous areas in the South of the UK express anxiety that "levelling up" will be at their expense as they contribute higher levels of tax but stand to lose public funding if it is redirected to the North. Without the commitment to such a mission, the UK government's "levelling up" agenda could once again fail to provide the necessary ambition and resource needed to tackle the longstanding and persistent problem of spatial inequalities.

6.4 REALIZING THE POTENTIAL OF PLACE IN POLICYMAKING

Paradoxically, this national "levelling up" mission depends on a recognition of the need for a radical move towards the more place-sensitive and place-based policy specified in Chapter 5. As we have seen, spatial policies in the UK have been dominated by the periodic reinvention and reworking of centrally orchestrated and spatially targeted programmes. The hope that such top-down policies can be modified in such a way as to radically help reduce spatial inequalities has proved remarkably robust, but has worn rather thin. A fundamentally stronger geographical sensitivity needs to be hard-wired into institutional design and policy formulation to make meaningful contributions to "levelling up". This stronger shift is key if the idea of "place" is to be made substantive across public policy rather than being an afterthought or bolt-on sound-bite. Building upon international work emphasizing the importance of "place-based" policy[29] and our distinctions between different forms of "place-sensitive" and "place-based" policy (Chapter 5), there is a need to go beyond establishing that place matters to further specify exactly how through its formal integration in institutions and policies.

As the analysis of the UK case illustrates, the level and nature of spatial socio-economic differentiation, complexity and polarization in the present era require a more geographically

https://doi.org/10.1080/2578711X.2021.1992172

sensitive approach to both diagnosing and responding to the general and particular issues faced by certain kinds of places. Yet, territorial development policy in the UK and elsewhere has been dominated in recent decades by a "city centrism" focused upon the geographical concentrations of economic activities in urban agglomerations. This approach has been further complicated in the UK case in England since the Brexit referendum by an explicit focus on towns.[30] As our analysis demonstrates, a wider geographical frame is needed to consider cities in concert with other geographies. Such a broader perspective would enable a better understanding of the predicaments and policy responses for particular groups of places.[31]

To be sure, there are some problems common to all or least most "left behind places", such as low skills and weak business formation ecosystems. Such common problems need a common policy response. But as we have shown, different types of "left behind places"—inner cities, former industrial cities, industrial towns, coastal areas, remote rural peripheries—also suffer from markedly different combinations of problems that demand a strongly differentiated and tailored mix of policy responses. There is now an international consensus that more research to better understand these variations and to target appropriate programmes on groups or clubs of such areas in "place-sensitive" ways is urgently required.[32]

In addition, a wide range of international work highlights the potential advantages of "place-based" approaches in economic and industrial strategy development, as they move beyond "one size fits all" or even centrally administered "place-sensitive" (place-differentiated) national policies. Place-based policymaking, formulated and implemented locally, can be explicitly diagnostic and focused on discovering exactly why individual local economies are failing to meet local needs and sustain social welfare.[33] There is now a menu of local development and place-based policies that have been evaluated and debated in the literature. Their key potential is that they are able to deliver initiatives that properly understand and meet the needs of local communities and economies, and moreover can adapt to these evolving needs as they change over time. These policies, for example, include those that focus on local firms and which aim to raise their productivity and quality through the provision of customized services and management, as well as fostering and facilitating research and technology cooperation between local small and medium-sized enterprises (SMEs).

Many local programmes have also shown the value of infrastructure investments and land and property supply that is relevant to local economic trajectories. In addition, the key potential of "Smart Specialisation" policies is they offer support to a process of local entrepreneurial discovery, which helps entrepreneurs as they develop innovations and start-ups and build on existing capabilities.[34] There is also, of course, an important set of place-based programmes that include investments in workers' skills and the provision of active labour market interventions in skills and training. A wide range of evidence indicates that effective skills and education policies need to be "joined up" and coordinated locally, particularly with measures to improve skills demand and utilization, and to anticipate and foster employment change.[35]

Such labour market programmes will be absolutely critical in "left behind places" as the dual impacts of automation and AI and the transition to a carbon-neutral economy continue to reshape labour demand. The key message of place-based policy is that there are strong limits on what we can predict in advance about the effectiveness of such policies in diverse settings. These programmes often work best in combination, which is best achieved through a collaborative and iterative design process that involves stakeholders at both local and national levels.[36]

While there is a large and, as yet, unrealized potential for many of these locally delivered and operationalized policies, it is clear that they cannot be effective without support from, and coordination with, political institutions at a variety of different scales. Placed-based policies require national institutional reform in order to enable, evaluate, regulate and fund their initiatives. Put simply, the outputs and cost-effectiveness of place-based levelling-up programmes will depend heavily on their alignment with the spatial consequences of mainstream government regulation and spending. Place-based policies and place sensitivity are mutually dependent. As a first step, meaningful decentralization of powers and resources are integral to enabling local discretion and sensitivity to local contexts and needs. That the UK has one of the highest levels of spatial economic inequality and one of the most centralized systems of economic, fiscal and political power is no mere coincidence. Local actors need the capacity, capability and resources to tailor their institutional arrangements and policy mixes to address their particular concerns. Any national mission for "levelling up" cannot be designed and delivered by national government alone. It is critical to involve not just local government but also local community-based organizations and third sector bodies in meaningful dialogue in the local economic development agenda, building on community-based assets and developing local skills.[37] Much has been learned about how to do this from the recently created Community Ownership Fund.

6.5 DECENTRALIZING TOWARDS A MULTILEVEL FEDERAL POLITY IN THE UK

A national mission for "levelling up" cannot, therefore, be delivered only from the centre of national government. It requires further, substantial and meaningful decentralization of powers and resources to move the UK in the direction of a multilevel, federal and experimentalist polity.[38]

Decentralization presents benefits and costs that require management between actors at different governance levels, especially the UK's asymmetric governance system (Table 6.2).

The challenge is to do this in such a way that delivers on the basic rationales for decentralization: better matching of public expenditure and services to local preferences; mobilization

https://doi.org/10.1080/2578711X.2021.1992172

Table 6.2 Benefits and costs of asymmetrical decentralization

Potential benefits	Potential costs
• Accommodate diverse preferences for autonomy across regions • Adapting the institutional and fiscal frameworks to the capacities of subnational governments • Advanced form of place-based policies • Experimenting • Sequencing decentralization • Providing the enabling institutional environment to design territorial development strategies more targeted to local needs • Tailoring solutions for special challenges	• Lack of accountability and transparency • Complexity and coordination costs • Lack of clarity for citizens • Potential risks of increased disparities (in capacities) • Secession and autonomy

Source: Adapted from Organisation for Economic Co-operation and Development (OECD).[39]

of local knowledge on economic potential and costs; and increased accountability of local governments to citizens by bringing decision-making and governance closer to the people.[40]

Devolution in Northern Ireland, Scotland and Wales has underpinned divergence in institutional and policy approaches to local, regional and urban development and planning.[41] Yet, such developments in how devolution should work are being challenged by centralized initiatives from the UK government at the national level, such as the Internal Market Bill, the new UK Shared Prosperity Fund replacement for EU regional policy in the post-Brexit period, and the establishment of freeports. Such moves are led by the current UK government's political imperative of attempting to preserve the UK Union and countering support for a further referendum on Scottish independence, managing relations with Northern Ireland and Ireland, and addressing emergent independence interests in Wales.[42] The key change needed is for the UK government to respect and enhance the particular settlements of powers and resources in each of the devolved territories—as well as the democratic concerns of citizens—rather than imposing further UK national-level centralization.

The problem of subnational development and governance is most acute and unresolved in England, the largest economic and demographic area in the UK. Finding an appropriate intermediate tier between the national and local in England has proved difficult historically. In the post-war period, the system has been characterized by a pendulum swinging between institutional arrangements at different spatial levels: regional to local, back to regional, then to local, then to subregional. The last decade has been marked by an ad-hoc, piecemeal and competitive deal-based approach that has created a patchwork of partially decentralized powers and resources across England.[43] Evaluation of the effectiveness of these arrangements has been limited.

Since 2020 in the post-Brexit and pandemic situation, the system in England has been overlaid by further differentiated allocation of powers and resources with multiple new national, competitive and relatively small-scale funds managed centrally and routed through local authorities: the Levelling Up Fund, Community Ownership Fund, Community Renewal Fund and Towns Fund. At the time of writing, details of the new UK Shared Prosperity Fund replacement for EU regional policy funding are yet to be confirmed. The nationally centralized allocation criteria, funds management and resources wasted in competitive bidding have all been raised as criticisms of the UK government's approach.[44]

Other recent policy developments have added further complexity and uncertainty to the institutional landscape. The Local Enterprise Partnerships, established in 2010 to replace the regional development agencies, which were criticized for being ineffective, expensive and not economically meaningful as areal units, have themselves proved highly problematic, concerning their purpose, number, geography, size, funding, and where they sit in the institutional architecture for local economic development and governance, especially in the light of the set of new combined local authority mayoral units that have been established. The lack of spatial coherence, constancy and integration of the UK's various territorial economic governance structures militates against effective long-term place-based policymaking. The contrast in this respect with, say, Germany could not be more striking.

What is needed, therefore, for a compelling national "levelling up" mission is a shift towards a more coherent and integrated governance system in England with meaningful decentralization of powers and resources. Guided by international experience and drawing on the Organisation for Economic Co-operation and Development's (OECD) (2019) decentralization principles, for example, a clearer purpose and direction needs to be set and a road map provided. Both a "levelling up" and "filling in" of powers and resources are required. Such a strategy, however, would need to work pragmatically with the existing governance patchwork and the geographically uneven moves towards unitarization and single-tier local authorities, as well as groupings of local authorities in combined structures either with or without directly elected mayors. Calls for such forms of a more comprehensive framework and "inclusive devolution" are being made elsewhere and seek to enable places to move forward according to their ambition, need and capacity.[45] Such governance structures would also need to find appropriate ways to involve and access the knowledge, experience, and skills of the private and civic sectors as well as citizens in accountable and transparent ways.

There is potential to focus on developing in England the kind of less centralized and multi-level governance system used in other comparable countries in three ways: (1) more formalized and integrated governance at local/subregional levels, building upon the combined authority models and geographies; (2) enabling and resourcing areas to coordinate for specific policy areas at particular geographical scales, for example, the Northern Powerhouse area for energy, transport and R&D infrastructures;[46] and (3) seeding capacity for parish and town councils to mobilize and address community-level issues.[47] The ambition would be to move towards a more coherent and integrated multilevel governance system, reducing complexity, perceived unfairness and confusion: a federated England in a multilevel devolved UK polity.

https://doi.org/10.1080/2578711X.2021.1992172

6.6 STRENGTHENING SUBNATIONAL FUNDING AND FINANCING

Vital to decentralized powers and resources are clear, sufficiently supported, and flexible funding and financing. Strengthening existing funding and financing tools is needed to ensure subnational actors have access to appropriate and adequate resources to support their local, regional and urban development. What is critical is to equip local actors with the tools to support long-term investment in support of recovery as part of the wider aim of government.[48]

There are public and private dimensions to the changes required. In the public sphere, first is the question of the appropriate level of resources. Here, the principle of "finance follows function" is needed to ensure that responsibilities assigned to different government levels are sufficiently funded.[49] Related to the magnitude of resources are their distribution and flexibility. Ironing out and ameliorating geographical inequities in the distribution of public funding is needed, especially in specific policy areas such as infrastructure.[50] Multi-year and flexible financial settlements enable subnational actors to formulate strategic, long-term and more transformational plans with appropriate funding and financing.

There is now a widespread view that the UK lags behind other advanced economies in the degree of decentralization of the public fiscal system. The UK has long had one of the lowest proportion of taxes that are raised and retained by local or regional governmental authorities.[51] In 2015, the government set out ambitions to allow local government to retain 100% of business rates by 2020. For various reasons, however, this has not happened and is now likely to be abandoned. The evidence from local 75% retention pilots suggests that if implemented at a full 100% retention, local councils could stand to benefit appreciably, though by virtue of their weaker economies many "left behind places" could be at a disadvantage. Other instruments for broadening local tax and finance-raising powers are also needed (e.g., new levies, capital allowances, localizing elements of national taxes). Such changes can be accompanied by enabling flexibilities within the existing system of tried-and-tested instruments as well as supporting innovation and experimentation with new funding and financing tools, especially for capital investment (Table 6.3).

These innovations can include new borrowing flexibilities and instruments skewed towards raising funds for investment in "left behind places", thereby contributing to the "levelling up" mission. Copying and supplementing the growing use of "green bonds", for example, new "levelling up bonds", could be issued for such purposes. Local and community municipal bonds have been successful in several countries, including the United States, Sweden and Denmark. In the United States, for example, local municipal bonds have long been used by states, cities and counties to raise funds for capital investment: in 2019, the local municipal bond market there stood at US$3.9 trillion (compared with a corporate bond market of US$9.6 trillion). There is also discussion to resurrect the Build America Bond market, which operated between 2009 and 2010. Both are being thought of as ways of funding the much-needed

Table 6.3 Subnational funding and financing tools

Temporality	Type	Examples
Established, tried and tested	Taxes and fees	Special assessments; user fees and tolls; other taxes
	Grants	Grant programmes (e.g., supranational, national, regional, city/city-regional, local)
	Debt finance	General obligation bonds; revenue bonds; conduit bonds; local municipal bonds; national loans funds (e.g., UK Public Works Loan Board)
	Tax incentives	New market, historic and housing tax credits; tax credit bonds; property tax relief; enterprise zones
	Developer fees	Impact fees; infrastructure levies
	Platforms for institutional investors	Pension and insurance infrastructure platforms; state infrastructure banks; regional infrastructure companies; real estate investment trusts; sovereign wealth funds
	Value capture mechanisms	Tax increment financing; special assessment districts; sales tax financing; infrastructure financing districts; community facilities districts; accelerated development zones
	Public–private partnerships	Private finance initiatives; build–(own)–operate–(transfer); build–lease–transfer; design–build–operate–transfer
	Asset leverage and leasing mechanisms	Asset leasing; institutional leasing; local asset-backed vehicles
Newer, innovative	Revolving infrastructure funds	Infrastructure trusts; investment recycling initiatives

Source: Adapted from Pike et al.[52]

upgrading and renewal of infrastructure across the country's communities.[53] In Sweden, the Kommuninvest agency, owned by 279 municipalities and 14 regions, accounts for over 40% of local municipal borrowing, equivalent to some £38 billion in 2020, and is rated AAA by both Standard & Poor and Moody. In the UK, a new UK Municipal Bonds Agency (UKMBA) was established in 2014 by a group of local authorities to boost their use of the debt markets to raise funds for capital projects, giving them a broader and cheaper source of finance than the loans available from the Public Works and Loan Board (PWLB).[54] Although slow to start, the UKMBA could become an important vehicle for expanding the local municipal bonds market, emulating the successful markets found elsewhere.

Such place-focused approaches to funding and financing have been explored, for example, in the UK "Total Place" pilots that sought to identify the multiple funding streams flowing into areas and improve their local leadership, alignment and coordination.[55] The initiatives generated a range of cost savings, improved policy outcomes and potential for further refinement.[56] Other work has identified how the specific and multiple funding streams from different Government departmental sources could be devolved and integrated into a "single pot" providing greater

https://doi.org/10.1080/2578711X.2021.1992172

autonomy and discretion to local and regional actors at the subnational level.[57] Adapting the International Monetary Fund's (IMF) national-level conception,[58] the overall aim is to increase the "fiscal space" for actors taxing and spending at the subnational level.

A key change is to move away from the model of local actors being forced to make ongoing competitive bids to national government centres. Such approaches reinforce centralized and top-down devised initiatives and criteria, further favour places that are already the best equipped with capacity and resources, and constitute "strategies for waste" through duplicated and wasted effort.[59] Crucially, in parallel to these subnational changes, there is a need to strengthen the underpinning national redistributive transfers and equalization systems to ensure areas with weaker economies and tax bases are not disadvantaged in more localized systems.[60]

The private sphere of funding and financing connects with longstanding calls to decentralize financial systems.[61] Here, the ambition is to widen sources of capital—including insurance groups, pension funds and sovereign wealth funds—and its forms—such as short, medium and longer term more "patient" kinds. Further potential changes include the re-establishment of local capital markets and promotion of mechanisms to stimulate local venture capital.[62]

Complementing such changes, there is developmental potential if the recently established and new institutions tasked with working between government and the private sector, including the British Business Bank and national UK Infrastructure Bank, are given more explicit geographical goals more closely tied to the national "levelling up" mission and more place-sensitive and place-based policy. This may require a more spatially biased and selective approach to the provision of finance to particular types of firms such as SMEs, to particular sectors and to "left behind places", for example, in terms of preferential lending rates and conditions. Such a change offers clear potential for a more coordinated and integrated approach across policy domains. Learning is available from the more regionalized development bank models that have been successful elsewhere, such as Finnvera in Finland, KfW in Germany and Strategic Banking Corporation of Ireland.[63] A local and place-making mission has also been proposed for the new Scottish National Investment Bank.[64]

In combination, these public and private dimensions need to be coordinated to provide enhanced autonomy, capacity and flexibility for actors at the subnational level to allow them to craft the "capital stack" of funding and financing to support long-term investment.[65] The capital stack refers to the mix of funding sources—including private, public grants and incentives, philanthropic, equity and debt—that are packaged together by local actors to provide the financing for specific investment programmes and projects (Table 6.4). Critical are the enabling powers and resources that underpin the capacity of local actors to exercise appropriate autonomy and discretion in this area.

Table 6.4 The "capital stack": five sources of funding for local investment

- Private funding
- Public grants and incentives
- Philanthropic donations
- Issuing equity
- Debt

Source: Adapted from Bamberger and Katz.[66]

6.7. EMBEDDING GEOGRAPHY IN THE NATIONAL STATE AND POLICY MACHINERY

A key step to enact this national "levelling up" mission is embedding geography more clearly and deeply in the national state and national policy machinery. As noted in Chapter 1, the ambition of "levelling up" is a long-term, multifaceted agenda that will involve marshalling the widest range of state capacities and resources over a sustained period.[67] Better focusing and coordinating national policy in more geographical ways is a prerequisite for making progress.

Each and every public policy has geographical expressions and implications, irrespective of whether policy is explicitly "spatial" or ostensibly "spatially blind" or "neutral". Macroeconomic policy such as interest rates impact different economic actors and activities in different places in varying ways. Reforms to national welfare policies reshape the geography of people's access to benefits and public services. Infrastructure policies shape the spatial distribution of essential systems and services across the country. As all public policies have geographical impacts and implications, the critical question is whether or not national governments choose to recognize and manage them. Our argument calls for a "spatialization" of state policy built upon the explicit and stronger recognition of this inherent geography.

There are lessons elsewhere of how national governments go some way towards encouraging this greater spatial sensitivity. For example, countries such as Austria and Germany use national spatial development concepts in the planning sphere.[68] Strategic spatial planning and the articulation, alignment and coordination of such plans is critically important in shaping the future pathways for economic, social and environmental development across the country. Matching with the national plans in the devolved territories and London, the UK2070 Commission has called for such a plan for England. The ways in which such guiding frameworks could be further developed, extended and strengthened as a steer across a wider set of national policy areas including and beyond strategic planning should be explored.

As Chapter 5 notes, the potential for the larger scale of expenditure by mainstream, but ostensibly non-geographical, government departments such as defence, education, health and welfare, typically far exceeds that of more explicitly spatial departments such as business, housing or local government. Indeed, such policies may act as "counter-regional" policies at specific times and work to reinforce rather than ameliorate spatial inequalities.[69] Hence, previous attempts in the UK to "bend the spend" and make such national policies more geographically aware and place sensitive have had disappointing and mixed results. Indeed, policy debates in the UK have raised concerns about changes in some departments such as education contributing to "levelling down" certain social groups and places rather than "levelling up".[70] Informed by work in the United States, and particularly by the Brookings Institution and Information Technology and Innovation Foundation,[71] UK national innovation and R&D policy too is struggling to reconcile its focus on excellence and geographical concentration in existing "hubs" in the so-called "Golden Triangle" (the London–Cambridge–Oxford area), with the need to promote new technology hubs and clusters in less prosperous regions.[72]

How, then, to make the national state and public policy more geographical? A longstanding approach is physically to decentralize the departments and agencies of the national state through public sector dispersal and relocation. There have been historical waves of such initiatives in the UK and elsewhere.[73] Indeed, as part of its "levelling up" agenda, the UK government has returned to this policy and established regional outposts for the finance ministry HM Treasury in Darlington in North East England, the Ministry of Housing, Communities and Local Government in Wolverhampton in the West Midlands, and the new national UK Infrastructure Bank in Leeds, Yorkshire. Such policies generate some benefits, although they are often overstated.[74] Future waves of public sector dispersal in support of a national "levelling up" mission need to be more substantive, systematic and longer term rather than ad hoc, piecemeal and short term. Merely moving a few hundred civil servants to Northern cities is unlikely seriously to reduce the London-centric nature of the UK governmental decision-making system. Changing the geography of the state will require a concerted dispersal of its institutions and the encouragement of better connections and deeper understanding of "the needs and aspirations of populations outside the metropolitan centre".[75]

Stronger institutional frameworks for coordinating and integrating policies will be essential prerequisites to a national mission of "levelling up" and reducing spatial inequalities. The aim should be to enable and deliver better alignment vertically between mainstream national and subnational policies and expenditure, and horizontally at each level through collaboration between public, private and civic actors. Harmonizing key and mainstream policy areas—such as education, health, housing and infrastructure—and skewing their aims and expenditure towards the needs of "left behind places" over a sustained period is vital. Critical too are information and knowledge flows between and across levels, countering top-down centralism with bottom-up localism within a multilevel system. As Chapter 1 explained, the UK government has used cross-governmental targets, for example, the public service agreements in England during the 2000s, but these have been stymied by departmentalism, and continued silo-style working has hampered more integration. Regional institutions too have been used in periods in the past, such as Government Offices for the regions in England in the 2000s, to provide coordination of national policies and a channel for regional issues to be communicated up to the centre. Learning from such initiatives to devise new forms of coordination and integration are integral to getting the state and its policymaking to operate in a more geographically aware and place-sensitive basis.

A further change is needed to provide stronger, more visible and senior political leadership befitting a clear and binding national mission for "levelling up". In the UK, this change would require leadership driven by the Prime Minister alongside a dedicated senior minister and even new department or Cabinet Office task force led and championed from the centre across government.[76]

Such leadership then needs to be supported by the deeper embedding of geography into the processes and procedures of policymaking throughout the state. This change needs to go beyond previous lighter touch efforts in the UK at "spatial proofing" policies for their effects at various scales, such as "rural proofing".[77] Hard-wiring greater spatial sensitivity into policymaking requires stronger mechanisms. Some progress has been made in strengthening HM Treasury's *Green Book* guidance on appraisal and evaluation to improve its recognition of social and spatial equity at a high level, but further efforts are required to embed its practical implementation.[78] A stronger spatial assessment of impacts could be integrated into HM Treasury's spending review processes and made a requirement in national departmental submissions for resources. As an analogue of the regulatory impact assessments needed for policies, another idea is to create "geographical impact assessments" as a binding way to make policymaking more explicitly geographical and place sensitive. This structured reporting would require policymakers to document the actual and potential geographical impacts and implications of policies. Such a change would necessarily require a more geographical perspective and act as a concrete step towards making policy more spatially sensitive and accountable against properly specified "levelling up" targets. If negative impacts are identified for particular kinds of places, then policies could be adapted or other compensating measures introduced. This idea also connects to longstanding concerns and ideas about how to improve the Whitehall civil service's spatial awareness.[79]

6.8 IMPROVING SUBNATIONAL STRATEGIC RESEARCH, INTELLIGENCE, MONITORING AND EVALUATION CAPACITY

Supporting and enhancing subnational policymaking capacity is critical to a more decentralized governance system and local, regional and urban contributions to the national "levelling up" mission.

https://doi.org/10.1080/2578711X.2021.1992172

Key learning points have been identified from the experience of Greater Manchester in England: developing an evidence-led approach is a long-term project; demand for evidence needs to be created; local partners need to be involved; external challenge should be encouraged; negative findings need to be acknowledged and addressed; compelling narratives need to be created built upon the evidence; evidence needs to be utilized and acted upon; and the development of evidence needs to focus upon long-term drivers of economic growth.[80] To these components we would add the need to broaden the focus of evidence to address social and environmental goals as well as economic objectives, and specific procedures for monitoring and evaluating policy, including learning from experiences elsewhere.

As argued above, having the appropriate powers and resources to exercise local autonomy and discretion is critical for deliberating and setting a vision for "development" and adapting and tailoring policy mixes to particular geographical situations in places. The need for such ambitions and aspirations is particularly timely amidst planning for economic recovery following the pandemic. New agendas need to be engaged and adapted to local, regional and urban circumstance including low carbon transition, digitization, Industry 4.0 and "good jobs".[81] Supporting local capacity and capability to identify, target and support such economic activities will be critical in strengthening the economic prospects of "left behind places".

The ability to experiment with policies in uncertain, particular and fast-changing contexts where no single actor has a monopoly on wisdom or insight into "what works" has been recognized as important by different approaches.[82] Various alternative economic development models are now attracting serious discussion, and all have relevance at the local, regional and urban scales, for example, anchor institutions,[83] community wealth-building,[84] "doughnut" economics,[85] the foundational economy,[86] inclusive growth[87] and the well-being economy.[88] Building upon and learning from early experimentations, combinations and assessments of such alternative development models, and their applicability and adaptation in different geographical contexts, will be integral to "levelling up".

6.9 CONCLUSIONS

A key message from our analysis is that there are a variety of different types of "left behind place" reflecting the different causal histories of local economic change and transformation, indicating that there needs to be similar differentiation in any policy programmes intended to "level up" those places. Economically lagging places can be found in every major British region, although there is undoubtedly a preponderance of "left behind places" in Northern regions, particularly the former old industrial cities and towns. Nevertheless, at the same time, some of the most problematic and slow-growth areas are also to be found among the inner London boroughs, and in some coastal and formerly industrial locations in the South. The number of these Southern areas is lower than those in the North, but their economic performance has been extremely poor and has continued to worsen. They should be an important part of a "levelling up" programme. The level of discontent caused by relative deprivation in relatively high-cost cities and regions is high.

"Levelling up policies" thus need to start by clearly distinguishing different types of "left behind" area, examining the ways in which social and economic conditions frustrate community and economy needs in each and, only then, devising a set of place-sensitive and targeted policies for these types of "clubs" of "left behind" areas. Some large city "left behind" districts have seen strong population growth from international migration, but most other types have seen very slow population growth due to internal outmigration. Policy needs to respond to these different conditions. Just as "left behind" problems are strongly differentiated, so policy responses need to be tailored and adapted to the needs of local economies. This can only be delivered by a radical expansion of "place-based" policymaking in the UK which allows national and local actors to collaborate on the design of appropriate targeted programmes.

Post-industrial economies are marked by a tendency to agglomeration in high-skilled and knowledge-intensive activities, and this is certainly evident in the UK, although it is not the only key locational process. The number of research-based concentrations of high-skilled activity has been limited and concentrated heavily in parts of London and neighbouring satellite cities (especially Oxford and Cambridge). Even in London the benefits have been seen far more in some boroughs than others. It is important to develop policies that spread the benefits from agglomeration and ensure that their income effects and innovations diffuse to the wider subregional economy and their firms (especially SMEs) and workers. There is a clear need for more policy thinking on how both can be achieved.

Many analyses of the predicaments of "left behind places" present a stark binary division between rapid growth in "winning" high-skilled cities and relative decline in "losing" areas. This oversimplifies the experience in Britain and indeed in other countries. A false binary distinction is presented to policymakers which offers only the possibility of growth in big cities and derived spillovers and other compensations elsewhere.

Our analysis shows that the post-industrial economy also involves a strong process of dispersal of activity and growth to smaller cities, towns and rural areas. This process has, however, been selective and has strongly discriminated between local areas, which is surprising given that the firms involved are in some ways more footloose than those that need to agglomerate in large cities. It is essential that policymaking also understands and engages with this second dynamic as it is likely to have been reinforced by the Covid-19 pandemic. It suggests that a strong "place-making" agenda focused on quality of life, infrastructure and housing in many "left-behind" areas would be important for post-industrial and service growth. However, a place-making agenda should not be defined as an immediate and superficial goal solely focused on town high-streets. Genuine place-making is a long-term process involving public and civic participation that allows local responses to those economic, environmental, and social constraints and problems that most strongly reduce the quality of life and extent of economic opportunity in local areas. The quality of infrastructure, housing stock and public services are crucial to the quality of place and the ability to secure and attract more dispersed forms of growth and employment. There is little hope of delivering "place-making" if public sector austerity is once again allowed to cut back public services more severely in poorer and more deprived areas.

Past policies have been underfunded, inconsistent, and inadequately tailored and adapted to the needs of different local economies. Resolving these issues requires substantially more decentralization of power and resources to place-based agencies. This would enable the "levelling up" programme to incorporate some of the many advantages of more "place-based" policymaking, and its potential ability to diagnose local problems, build on local capabilities and adapt to local changes in circumstances. Our findings outline a number of principles and preconditions for the enabling and funding of more "place-based" policymaking. Crucially these place-based efforts need to be coordinated and aligned with "place-sensitive" mainstream national policies. The key challenge for a "levelling up" mission is to integrate "place-based" policies with greater place sensitivity in national policies and in regulation and mainstream spending, and this will require the reform of priorities and institutions at a national scale. In the past, the two have been uncoordinated and have rarely been aligned, indeed the former have frequently been swamped and undermined by the latter. Resolving this misalignment will be critical to the success of a "levelling up" agenda.

In summary, our recommendations are that the UK government should:

- Grasp the transformative moment for local, regional and urban development policy as the UK adjusts to a post-Covid world and seeks a net zero carbon future.

- Establish a clear and binding national mission for "levelling up".

- Realize the potential of place in policymaking.

- Decentralize towards a multilevel federal polity in the UK.

- Strengthen subnational funding and financing and adopt new financing models involving the public, private sector and civic sectors to generate the resources required.

- Embed geography in the national state and in national policy machinery.

- Improve subnational strategic research, intelligence, monitoring and evaluation capacity.

A failure to learn from the lessons of the last 70 years would mean the UK becoming an ever more divided nation with all the associated economic, social and political costs, risks and challenges that this presents.[89]

NOTES

1   Collier P (2018) *The Future of Capitalism: Facing the New Anxieties*. London: Allen Lane, at 152–153.

2   Sandbu M (2020) *The Economics of Belonging: A Radical Plan to Win Back the Left Behind and Achieve Prosperity for All*. Princeton: Princeton University Press.

3   There are also other major trends and developments that will have profound uneven implications for regions, cites and localities in the advanced economies, including demographic ageing, historically high levels of public debt, and imbalances and conflicts that characterize the global trading system. On the latter, see, for example, Pettis M (2013) *The Great Rebalancing: Trade, Conflict and the Perilous Road Ahead for the World Economy*. Princeton: Princeton University Press; and Rodrik D (2018) *Straight Talk on Trade: Ideas for a Sane World Economy*. Princeton: Princeton University Press.

4   UK in a Changing Europe (2021) *Brexit and Beyond: Policy*. UK in a Changing Europe. https://ukandeu. ac.uk/wp-content/uploads/2021/02/87864-Brexit-and-Beyond-Policy.pdf/.

5   Delwaide J (2011) The return of the state? *European Review*, 19: 69–91.

6   Gray M and Barford A (2018) The depths of the cuts: The uneven geography of local government austerity. *Cambridge Journal of Regions, Economy and Society*, 11: 541–563; Lobao L, Gray M, Cox K and Kitson M (2018). The shrinking state? Understanding the assault on the public sector. *Cambridge Journal of Regions, Economy and Society*, 11: 389–408.

7   In most countries, the drop in gross domestic product (GDP) in the second quarter of 2020 was dramatic. Compared with the same quarter in 2019, GDP fell by 20.4% in the UK, 12.4% in the Eurozone, 10.4% in the G7 and 10.5% in the Organisation for Economic Co-operation and Development (OECD); *Economic Indicators, No. 02784, January 2021*. London: House of Commons.

8   See https://www.mckinsey.com/~/media/McKinsey/Industries/Public%20Sector/Our%20Insights/ The%2010%20trillion%20dollar%20rescue%20How%20governments%20can%20deliver%20 impact/The-10-trillion-dollar-rescue-How-governments-can-deliver-impact-vF.pdf/.

9   Agnew J and Entrikin JN (2004) Introduction: The Marshall Plan as model and metaphor. In J Agnew and JN Entrikin (eds.), *The. Marshall Plan Today: Model and Metaphor*, pp. 1–22. London: Routledge.

10 Organisation for Economic Co-operation and Development (OECD) (2020) *Building Back Better: A Sustainable, Resilient Recovery after COVID-19*. Paris: OECD.

11 Climate Change Committee (2020) *COVID-19 Can Be An Historic Turning Point in Tackling the Global Climate Crisis*, 25 June. https://www.theccc.org.uk/2020/06/25/covid-19-can-be-an-historic-turning-point-in-tackling-the-global-climate-crisis/; Mazzucato M (2020) *Covid-19 and the Green New Deal*, 1 December. United Nations, Department of Economic and Social Affairs blog. https://www.un.org/ development/desa/undesavoice/more-from-undesa/2020/12/50538.html/.

12 Tankersley J (2021) Biden to propose $6 trillion budget to make U.S. more competitive. *The New York Times*, 17 June. https://www.nytimes.com/2021/05/27/business/economy/biden-plan.html/.

13 Beatty C, Fothergill S and Powell R (2007) Twenty years on: Has the economy of the UK coalfields recovered? *Environment and Planning A: Economy and Space*, 39: 1654–1675.

14 Mellish T, Luzmore N and Shahbaz A (2020). Why were the UK and USA unprepared for the COVID-19 pandemic? The systemic weaknesses of neoliberalism: A comparison between the UK, USA, Germany, and South Korea. *Journal of Global Faultlines*, 7: 9–45.

[15] For example, House of Commons Business, Energy and Industrial Strategy Committee (2021) *Post-Pandemic Economic Growth: Levelling Up*, 26 July (HC 566).

[16] HM Government (2021) *Building Back Better: Our Plan for Growth*, London: HM Government.

[17] New Economics Foundation (2008) *Green New Deal*. London: New Economics Foundation.

[18] See Chapters 2–4; see also Bristow G and Healey A (eds.) (2018) *Economic Crisis and the Resilience of Regions: A European Study*. Cheltenham: Edward Elgar; Martin RL, Bailey D, Evenhuis E, Gardener B, Pike A, Sunley P and Tyler P (2019) *The Economic Performance of Britain's Cities: Patterns, Processes and Policy Implications* (Economic and Social Research Council (ESRC) Structural Transformation, Adaptability and City Economic Evolutions Research Project). www.cityevolutions.org.uk; Martin RL and Gardiner B (2021) The policy challenges of levelling up. In C Berry, J Froud and T Barker (eds.), *The Political Economy of Industrial Strategy in the UK*, pp. 215–234. Newcastle upon Tyne: Agenda.

[19] For example, Coyle D and Sensier M (2020) The imperial treasury; Appraisal methodology and regional economic performance in the UK. *Regional Studies*, 44: 283–295.

[20] See https://www.theguardian.com/politics/2009/oct/06/michael-white-conservative-conference-diary/.

[21] Martin RL, Gardiner B and Tyler P (2011) Does spatial agglomeration increase national growth? Evidence from the European Union. *Journal of Economic Geography*, 11: 979–1006.

[22] Mazzucato M and Dibb G (2019) *Missions: A Beginner's Guide* (Policy Brief, December). Institute for Innovation and Public Purpose (IIPP). https://www.ucl.ac.uk/bartlett/public-purpose/sites/public-purpose/files/iipp_policy_brief_09_missions_a_beginners_guide.pdf/.

[23] Mazzucato and Dibb (2019), see Reference 22.

[24] Mazzucato and Dibb (2019), see Reference 22.

[25] Centre for Cities (2021) *So You Want to Level Up?* London: Centre for Cities; Onward (2020) *Measuring Up for Levelling Up*. London: Onward.

[26] Centre for Cities (2021), see Reference 25; Local Trust (2019) *Left Behind? Understanding Communities on the Edge*. London: Local Trust.

[27] Organisation for Economic Co-operation and Development (OECD) (2019) *Making Decentralisation Work: A Handbook for Policymakers*. Paris: OECD.

[28] Tomaney J and Pike A (2021) Levelling up? *Political Quarterly*, 91: 43–48.

[29] Beer A, McKenzie F, Blažek J, Sotarauta M and Ayres S (2020) *Every Place Matters: Towards Effective Place-Based Policy* (RSA Policy Impact Book Series). London: Routledge.

[30] Jennings W and Stoker G (2019) The divergent dynamics of cities and towns: Geographical polarisation and Brexit. *Political Quarterly*, 90(S2): 155–166.

[31] Iammarino S, Rodríguez-Pose A and Storper M (2018) Regional inequality in Europe: Evidence, theory and policy implications. *Journal of Economic Geography*, 19: 273–298.

[32] Bartik TJ (2020) Using place-based jobs policies to help distressed communities. *Journal of Economic Perspectives*, 34: 99–127.

[33] Rodrik D and Sabel C (2019) *Building a Good Jobs Economy* (Working Paper). Harvard. https://drodrik.scholar.harvard.edu/publications/building-good-jobs-economy/.

[34] Foray D, Eichler M and Keller M (2020) Smart Specialisation Strategies—Insights gained from a unique European policy experiment on innovation and industrial policy design. *Review of Evolutionary Political Economy*, 2: 83–103.

[35] Froy F and Giguère S (2010) *Putting in Place Jobs that Last: A Guide to Rebuilding Quality Employment at Local Level* (Local Economic and Employment Development (LEED) Working Papers). Paris: Organisation for Economic Co-operation and Development (OECD).

[36] Barca F (2009) *An Agenda for a Reformed Cohesion Policy* (Independent report prepared at the request of Danuta Hubner, Commissioner for Regional Policy); Beer et al. (2020), see Reference 29.

[37] Plumb N, McNabola A and Alakeson V (2021). *Backing Our Neighbourhoods: Making Levelling Up Work by Putting Communities in the Lead*. London: Power to Change; Tyler P (2019) *Regenerating Left Behind Places: Lessons from the Past*. Cambridge: Department of Land Economy, University of Cambridge. https://www.landecon.cam.ac.uk/system/files/documents/left-behind-tyler-august-2019.pdf/.

[38] Morgan K and Sabel C (2019) The experimentalist polity. In *Radical Visions of Future Government*, pp. 75–81. London, National Endowment for Science, Technology and the Arts (NESTA).

[39] OECD (2019) *Asymmetric Decentralisation: Policy Implications in Colombia*. Paris: OECD.

[40] Tomaney J, Pike A, Torissi G, Tselios V and Rodríguez-Pose A (2011) *Decentralisation Outcomes: A Review of Evidence and Analysis of International Data* (Report for the Department of Communities and Local Government: London).

[41] St. Denny E (2016) *What Does It Mean for Public Policy to be 'Made in Wales'?* LSE BPP blog, 19 October. https://blogs.lse.ac.uk/politicsandpolicy/what-does-it-mean-for-public-policy-to-be-made-in-wales/; Trench A (ed.) (2007) *Devolution and Power in the United Kingdom*. Manchester: Manchester University Press.

[42] Paun A (2018) *Saving the Union from Brexit Will Require Bold Thinking about the Constitution*, 13 September, IfG blog. https://www.instituteforgovernment.org.uk/blog/saving-union-brexit-will-require-bold-thinking-about-constitution/.

[43] Pike A, Kempton L, Marlow D, O'Brien P and Tomaney J (2016) *Decentralisation: Issues, Principles and Practice*. Newcastle upon Tyne: Centre of Urban and Regional Development Studies (CURDS), Newcastle University.

[44] Fothergill S and Gore T (2021) *Plan for the North: How to Deliver the Levelling Up that's Really Needed*. Sheffield: Centre for Regional Economic and Social Research, Sheffield Hallam University.

[45] UK2070 Commission (2021) *Make No Little Plans: Acting at Scale for a Fairer and Stronger Future*. London: UK2070 Commission.

[46] MacKinnon D (2020) Governing uneven development: The Northern Powerhouse as a "state spatial strategy". *Territory, Politics, Governance*, 9(5), 613–635.

[47] Wills J (2016) *Locating Localism: Statecraft, Citizenship and Democracy*. Bristol: Policy Press.

[48] Fothergill and Gore (2021), see Reference 44.

49 OECD (2019), see Reference 27.

50 Pike A, O'Brien P, Strickland T, Thrower G and Tomaney J (2019) *Financialising City Statecraft and Infrastructure*. Cheltenham: Elgar.

51 Martin RL, Pike A, Tyler P and Gardiner B (2016) Spatially rebalancing the UK economy: Towards a new policy model? *Regional Studies, 50*, pp. 342–357.

52 Pike et al. (2019), see Reference 50.

53 See https://www.brookings.edu/blog/up-front/2021/08/04/what-are-build-america-bonds-or-direct-pay-municipal-bonds/.

54 See https://www.localis.org.uk/wp-content/uploads/2015/09/loc_municipal_bonds_web.pdf/. The PWLB was in fact abolished in 2020 and its functions transferred to HM Treasury, where they are administered through the UK Debt Management Office.

55 HM Treasury and Communities and Local Government (2010) *Total Place: A Whole-Area Approach to Public Services*. London: HM Treasury and Communities and Local Government.

56 National Audit Office (NAO) (2013) *Case Study on Integration: Measuring the Costs and Benefits of Whole-Place Community Budgets*. London: NAO.

57 Heseltine M (2012) *No Stone Unturned in Pursuit of Growth*. London: Department for Business, Innovation and Skills.

58 International Monetary Fund (IMF) (2018) *Assessing Fiscal Space: An Update and Stocktaking*, 15 June. Washington, DC: IMF.

59 Rodríguez-Pose A and Wilkie C (2018) Strategies of gain and strategies of waste: What determines the success of development intervention? *Progress in Planning*, 133. https://www.sciencedirect.com/science/article/abs/pii/S0305900618300047/.

60 McKay R (2001) Regional taxing and spending: The search for balance. *Regional Studies*, 35: 563–575.

61 Klagge B, Martin R and Sunley P (2017) The spatial structure of the financial system and the funding of regional business: A comparison of Britain and Germany. In R Martin and J Pollard (eds.), *Handbook on the Geographies of Money and Finance*, pp. 125–155. Cheltenham: Edward Elgar.

62 Gardiner B and Martin RL (2019) There could be a case for more localised capital markets. *Public Finance*, 14 June. https://www.publicfinance.co.uk/opinion/2019/06/there-could-be-case-more-localised-capital-markets/.

63 Michie R and Wishlade F (2014) *Business Development Banks and Funds in Europe: Selected Examples*. Glasgow: European Policies Research Centre, University of Strathclyde.

64 Mazzucato M and Macfarlane L (2019) *A Mission-Oriented Framework for the Scottish National Investment Bank*. London: UCL Institute for Innovation and Public Purpose.

65 Bamberger L and Katz B (2019) *How Financial Innovation Can Enable Inclusive Opportunity Zones*. https://drexel.edu/nowak-lab/publications/reports/voices-from-the-field/.

66 Bamberger and Katz (2019), see Refence 64.

67 Institute for Fiscal Studies (IFS) (2020) *Levelling Up: Where and How?* London: IFS.

[68] In Austria, the *Österreicche Raumordnungskonferenz* (Spatial Planning and Development Conference) coordinates national strategies and the territorial development interests of different spatial levels (states, cities and municipalities). In Germany, the *Geminschaftsaufgabe Verbesserung der Regionalen Wirtschaftsstuktur* (Joint Task Improvement of Regional Structures) brings together the federal government and state (regional) governments to set out an annual framework plan, with a calibrated voting system to ensure consensus across levels of government.

[69] This phrase was used by Lord Heseltine in the 1980s to draw attention to the fact that UK government spending on defence and public purchasing, which greatly exceeds that on regional policy, tends to favour the more prosperous areas of the country, thereby effectively countering the impact of the regional aid intended to support economically lagging regions.

[70] IFS (2020), see Reference 67.

[71] Atkinson RD, Muro M and Whiton J (2019) *The Case for Growth Centers: How to Spread Tech Innovation across America*. Washington, DC: Brookings Institution.

[72] Forth T and Jones R (2021) *The Missing £4bn: Making R&D Work for the Whole UK*. London: National Endowment for Science, Technology and the Arts (NESTA); UK2070 Commission (2021), see Reference 45.

[73] Marshall JN, Bradley D, Hodgson C, Alderman N and Richardson R (2005) Relocation, relocation, relocation: Assessing the case for public sector dispersal. *Regional Studies*, 39: 767–787.

[74] Nickson S, Mullens-Burgess E and Thomas A (2020) *Moving Out: Making a Success of Civil Service Relocation*. London: Institute for Government.

[75] Rycroft P (2020) The civil service survived Dominic Cummings. Now comes the hard bit. *Prospect*, 18(November).

[76] The recent establishment of a Levelling Up Unit in the Cabinet Office is a potentially useful step in this direction. As this book was being submitted for publication, a new Secretary of State for Housing, Communities and Local Government was appointed, who is also to be in charge of the government's "levelling up" agenda for the UK, although precisely what his remit and powers will be are unknown.

[77] Department for Environment, Food and Rural Affairs (DEFRA) (2017) *Rural Proofing*. London: DEFRA.

[78] Smith C (2021) *Government Investment Programmes: The "Green Book"*, 17 March. House of Lords Library Blog. https://lordslibrary.parliament.uk/government-investment-programmes-the-green-book/.

[79] Hope N and Leslie C (2009) *Challenging Perspectives: Improving Whitehall's Spatial Awareness*. London: New Local Government Network.

[80] Harding A and Holden J (2015) *Using Evidence: Greater Manchester Case Study*. London: What Works Centre for Local Economic Growth.

[81] de Propris L and Bailey D (2020) *Industry 4.0 and Regional Transformations*. London: Routledge; New Economics Foundation (2021) *Powering the Just Transition*. London: New Economics Foundation; Rodrik D and Sabel C (2019) *Building a Good Jobs Economy* (Working Paper). Harvard. https://drodrik.scholar.harvard.edu/publications/building-good-jobs-economy/.

[82] Foundational Economy Collective (2020) *The Foundational Approach*. https://foundationaleconomy.com/introduction/; Kaufman M (2018) *Four Lessons from Our Policy Evaluation Experiments*, 15

June. What Works Centre for Local Economic Growth blog. https://whatworksgrowth.org/blog/four-lessons-from-our-policy-evaluation-experiments/.

[83] Katz B and Wagner J (2014) *The Rise of Innovation Districts: A New Geography of Innovation in America* (Metropolitan Policy Program). Washington, DC: Brookings Institution.

[84] CLES (2021) *Community Wealth Building: A History*. Manchester: CLES.

[85] Raworth K (2017) *Doughnut Economics: Seven Ways to Think Like a 21st Century Economist*. London: Cornerstone.

[86] Foundational Economy Collective (2020), see Reference 82.

[87] Lee N (2019) Inclusive growth in cities: A sympathetic critique. *Regional Studies*, 53: 424–434.

[88] Chrysopoulou A (2020) The vision of a well-being economy. *Stanford Social Innovation Review*, 16(December).

[89] De Ruyter A, Martin RL and Tyler P (2021). Geographies of discontent: Sources, manifestations and consequences. *Cambridge Journal of Regions, Economy and Society*, 14(3), 381–393; Evenhuis E, Lee N, Martin RL and Tyler P (2021) Rethinking the political economy of place: Challenges of productivity and inclusion. *Cambridge Journal of Regions, Economy and Society*, 14: 3–24.

REGIONAL STUDIES POLICY IMPACT BOOKS

The RSA's Policy Impact Books form a series of short policy facing books addressing issues of contemporary concern.

The books in this series are commissioned to address topical policy questions of contemporary importance to communities engaged in regional and urban studies issues.

 @regstud

 @RegionalStudiesAssociation

 Regional Studies Association

 office@regionalstudies.org

 www.regionalstudies.org